DON'T PAY RETAIL!

Indiana's Discount Buying Guide

By

Regina Miller
Jennifer Mixer

Guild Press of Indiana, Inc.
6000 Sunset Lane
Indianapolis, IN 46208

Printed in the United States of America

Library of Congress
Catalog Card Number
94-79566

ISBN 1-878208-54-3

TABLE OF CONTENTS OVERVIEW

TABLE OF CONTENTS

INTRODUCTION

This book is a guide to discount shopping in Metropolitan Indianapolis and surrounding areas with state-wide coverage of factory outlets and manufacturer marketplaces. Expect to find savings of hundreds on everything from antiques to health foods. If you can still read this a year from now then you haven't used the book to its fullest potential! Keep a copy in your car so it will be at hand whenever the urge to save money strikes. When used properly, the book will be torn, tattered and chocolate-covered and will have earned its weight in gold by the next edition. Businesses included did not pay for inclusion in this guide; selections are at the authors' discretion, as is descriptive information.

Who is Included?

The establishments listed in this book fall into at least one of the following categories:

- Stores Selling Below Suggested List Price
- Manufacturer's Outlets and Malls
- Discounted Services
- Resale Stores
- Stores with Unusually Large Selection or Inventory
- Stores Offering Substantial Discounts
- Unique Items
- Inexpensive or Free Local Attractions
- Discounted Mail-Order Companies

Discount Coupons

Stores listed with an asterisk at the end of their name offer additional savings to DON'T PAY RETAIL! bookholders. The final selection of stores to be included in the book was made before coupon space was offered to insure impartiality in choosing entries. Simply clip the store's coupon from the back of the book and present it for additional savings!

Things To Do

We have included a special section of "things to do," for all of those people, like ourselves, who have fallen into a rut. This section is by no means a complete list of things to do in Indiana or even Indianapolis, but it's a good spot to browse. The next time you have the afternoon off with nothing to do, flip through this section, and maybe, just maybe, it will get you out of the living room and into the car. Many of the places included have discounts on certain days or season passes that can save you a bundle.

If You Can't Find It...

Keep looking! Some stores are entered in more than one category. Many of the categories overlap and because of space limitations not every store is listed in all of the categories that it could be. Think of other products that may be sold along with the item you are looking for and look those up. If all else fails scan the Table of Contents to see if it's there—then if you can't find your item or store, pick up a pencil, write to us and give us a piece of your mind!

Notes to Reader

We Want To Hear From You!

If you know of any other great bargains, please send us their names, addresses and telephone numbers so we can include them in the next edition. Also, we would like to hear about your experiences with the establishments already included. While we cannot resolve problems with these stores, we will keep any complaints on file for reference for future editions. Please send your comments and suggestions to:

Don't Pay Retail!
P.O. Box 47554
Indpls., IN 46247-0554

Additional copies can be obtained from your local bookstore or by completing the form at the back of the book and returning it to the above address.

Authors' Note

While we have visited or contacted almost all of the included establishments ourselves, we are not responsible for any misinformation or changes in information or policies since publication. We suggest calling ahead to see if the store is indeed still open, and in the same location, and that all other pertinent information remains the same. Stores were chosen based on the authors' research, interviews with local consumers, and by information supplied by the businesses themselves. This book is solely a guide and does not imply endorsement of any establishment included.

Merchants

Stand up and be counted! We can't include you if we can't find you. If you feel the heavens are frowning on you because you have unjustly been left out, write and let us know. As long as you can save our readers their hard earned money (and meet a few very minimal criteria), we'll include you in the next edition.

Legend

Location Information

The telephone number and the address, including zip code, is provided in most instances. Stores with six or fewer locations have all locations listed. Stores with more than six locations are listed with one address and telephone number. Other locations can be obtained by calling the location listed or by consulting a telephone directory. Stores with locations in outlet malls have the phone number and name of the outlet center listed only. Addresses of the outlet center can be found in the Outlet Mall Directory at the back of the book. Hours and other information may vary from one location to another, so save time by calling ahead.

Methods of Payment

Many stores accept major credit cards or their own store-issued credit card in addition to cash. Personal checks are accepted with proper ID (usually a driver's license and/or a major credit card) at many establishments. Again, call ahead regarding each store's policy.

Stores Accepting Coupons

Stores offering additional savings in the form of a coupon in the special "coupon section" are indicated with an asterisk (*) following the store's name. The amount of discount is printed on the coupon.

BARGAIN BUYING TACTICS: BE TIME AND MONEY AHEAD

General Strategies

• When shopping for a particular item, especially big-ticket items, visit a couple of stores ahead of time to learn more about the product itself. When choosing the model which has the features you want, use a buying guide (like "Consumer Reports") to aid you in your decision-making.

• Don't be afraid to use the phone! Call ahead and see if the stores have the item, whether or not it's in stock, and what the price is. If they won't tell you the price over the phone (some discount places won't in order to encourage you to come in), tell them the lowest price you have found so far and ask if they can beat it.

• Check on price-matching and price-beating guarantees. Even if the price is slightly higher in your neighborhood store, many stores have price matching policies that may save you a trip across town. Also, if prices are about the same everywhere you have checked, look for stores with price-beating policies. Many stores will not only match prices, but also beat them by a certain percentage. Some stores will call the store where you found the better price to verify it, others insist on having a copy of the item with its price in print in form of an advertisement or in writing from the store. Check the policies ahead of time to save unnecessary trips.

• Are you spending more in gas than you stand to save on the product? If you're only going to save a dollar or two on an item, don't drive all over town to get it!

• Is it really a good deal? Asking yourself if you want or need an item and will use it is the first gauge of whether or not it's a good deal. If you're just shopping for the sake of shopping, go someplace where you know you won't run the risk of spending more than what you intended.

Also when deciding if it's a good deal, make sure you are comparing apples to apples. Are the products really the same? When the prices are close, decide which features are most important and look for subtle differences like warranties and return policies.

• Check the store's reputation with the Better Business Bureau. Ask friends about their experiences.

• Sign up for mailing lists at your favorite stores. Often times you will get advance notification of sales and special events. One precautionary note: if you don't like to get junk mail ask ahead of time if the list is given to any outside agencies or other stores.

• Know what presents you need to buy each year. Keep a small note book of important information, like sizes, favorite colors, and hobbies of each person. Grab it on your way out to go shopping and when you see something that's an exceptional value worth storing until the event, buy it. Be sure to put it someplace where you can locate it—it's not a good value if you never find it again!

• It doesn't hurt to ask! Some discount stores will negotiate price while others won't. Even if the price isn't negotiable, the terms may be. You may be able to get extra features, equipment or warranties at a discount simply by negotiating them in with the price they have quoted you. Even stores that wouldn't normally negotiate at all will often give you a discount on an item that has a blemish or small defect if you point it out and ask if they can discount it.

• Always ask about return policies and money-back guarantees. On bigger ticket items be sure to get it in writing.

• Know what you are buying. Even if a product costs a little less, if it turns out not to work as well as a more expensive brand or to hold up for an acceptable length of time then it's not a good bargain. Buying the cheapest product doesn't insure getting the best value. Sometimes paying a little more for a product that may last twice as long is worth the extra money. Conversely, just because you pay more for an item doesn't necessarily mean it's better. Knowing what quality you are looking for and what quality you are buying, all at the best price, is the only way to be sure you're getting a bargain.

• Establish a relationship with your favorite stores. Use sales people that you like again and again. It's a great way to get personalized service and sound advice, plus, if you ever should have a problem, the store should be very eager to satisfy a repeat customer.

Resale Strategies

• Follow above General Strategies that apply.

• When shopping resale stores, start by visiting many of them. Once you find a few that carry the brands you like at the great savings you'll enjoy, frequent them often. Many have consistent policies on what brand and condition of merchandise they will accept and get new arrivals almost on a daily basis. Know what you're looking for. For example, are you looking for good school clothes or play clothes for your child? The condition of merchandise from one resale store to another may vary greatly, just as prices do.

• Don't overlook resale stores as a place to get rid of your unwanted items. You're likely to get more than you would for an item in a yard sale—and what a great way to recycle!

Mail-Order Strategies

• Follow above General Strategies that apply.

• When you can, order small, inexpensive amounts to begin with to test whether or not you like the store's products and policies.

• Ask for references in your area. Most mail-order companies will be more than happy to supply you with a few names and phone numbers of local satisfied customers. Call and see how happy they are with the company. Just keep in mind that the company isn't likely to give you names of customers from their complaint files!

• Before returning anything to a mail-order company contact them and ask for their return procedures. It's a good idea to find this out before ordering. When returning an item, be sure to let the company know the product is on its way back.

• In case there is a problem with a mail order, contact the company immediately. If the company refuses to handle the complaint and resolve the problem in a fair manner, contact your local U.S. Post Office and ask for instructions on dealing with a mail-order company complaint.

• Don't forget! As appetizing as it may sound when a catalogue advertises that out-of-state customers do not need to include sales tax, remember Indiana still expects you to pay sales tax on the item when you fill out your taxes at the end of the year!

III
Directory
of
Stores and Services

ANTIQUES & COLLECTIBLES

ANDERSON ANTIQUE MALL
1407 Main St.
Anderson, IN 46016
800/427-4121

Everything for the antique enthusiast, from collector decorating items to furniture. The Anderson Antique Mall has over 70 shops, and is open seven days a week. They buy and sell antique items and collectibles.

ANTIQUE MALL OF CARMEL
622 S. Range Line Rd.
Carmel, IN 46032
317/848-1280

Over 30 booths of quality antiques available to the public seven days a week.

COLONIAL ANTIQUES
5000 W. 96th
Indianapolis, IN 46268
317/873-2727

Looking for that authentic piece to recapture the history of your home? This is the place that specializes in architectural antiques. If you have items to sell, they buy "a wide variety of antique items—any quantity."

FLEALESS MARKET
2010 E. 46th St.
Indianapolis, IN 46205
317/923-8135

Flealess features upscale, gently used merchandise ranging from decor and daily household items to antiques, collectibles, glassware and furniture. Expect to see savings around 30 to 50% or more below retail. The Flealess Market strives to be a cut above the everyday, run-of-the-mill flea market. Prices can be reasonably negotiated, and their layaway policy is geared towards you. There is no layaway fee and no time limit, only regular payments are required. There's a different sale each day and Seniors can save even more on Tuesdays. Cleanliness and customer satisfaction are at the top of their priorities and they pride themselves on the special attention given to the needs of women.

FOUNTAIN SQUARE ANTIQUE MALL

1056 Virginia Ave.
Indianapolis, IN 46203
317/636-1056

Fountain Square Antique Mall buys items straight out to offer for sale or they will sell them on consignment. Over seventy booths are featured in this two-story mall which brings together quite a collection of everything from beautiful antique furniture to Norman Rockwell collectible plates. If you have items to sell, they'll "buy one item or an entire household." Appraisal service is also available.

INDIANAPOLIS DOWNTOWN ANTIQUE MALL

1044 Virginia Ave.
Indianapolis, IN 46203
317/635-5336

Located in Historical Fountain Square, in what is rapidly becoming an Antique Alley, Indianapolis Downtown Antique Mall has over forty shops under one roof. Among their wares are: Depression Glass, Nippon, Hummels, American art pottery, furniture, jewelry, and handmade quilts. Their maroon awning makes them easy to find. They're open daily, Mastercard and Visa are accepted. Special discounts are given to frequent buyers and dealers. Layaway is available.

LAZY ACRE ANTIQUES

St. Rd. 32 West
Noblesville, IN 46060
317/773-7387

A person could get lost here, in 10,000 square feet of antiques! "City Antiques at country prices" is what they promote; choose from a wide selection of English pine furniture, glassware, gifts, wicker and more.

NATIONAL STEEL CRAFTERS OF INDIANAPOLIS

3523 W. US Rt.40
Greenfield, IN 46040
317/359-6000

Having trouble adding that final touch to your antique home? At National Steel you can get an antique stove or fireplace insert to add the perfect finishing touch to your home.

NORTH INDY ANTIQUE MALL

7226 N. Corporation Dr.
Fishers, IN 46258
317/578-2671

North Indy Antique Mall has over 8,000 square feet of antiques and collectibles. Items are well organized and the staff is friendly and helpful.

RESTORATION SERVICES

970 Fort Wayne Ave.
Indianapolis, IN 46202
317/632-7161

Restoration Antiques is an architectural salvage, antique, and curio store that occupies the Buschmann Building, a National Historic Landmark. They sell a variety of salvage items for restoration projects, designers and collectors. Tim and Billy, the owners, also restore historic homes in the Indianapolis area and offer consultation on such projects. It's a very unique, ever-changing "architectural salvage paradise." Ask about their refund and layaway policy. Discounts are offered to people in the trade.

SARVER'S ANTIQUE ORIENTAL RUGS
2602 E. 62nd
Indianapolis, IN 46220
317/255-3066

Quality antique Oriental Rugs are in abundance here. Oriental Rugs will add more than a touch of class when blended with other antiques or even standing alone as the centerpiece of your decor.

WELCOME HOUSE ANTIQUES, ETC.
202 E. Main St.
Westfield, IN 46074
317/867-0077

Affordable prices on antiques, collectibles, and quality resale merchandise. The inventory includes furniture, pictures, dishware, crafts, wrought iron, rugs and more. Stop by Wednesday, Friday or Saturday. If those days don't fit your schedule, Welcome House Antiques is more than happy to accept appointments.

APPLIANCES

≺ NEW & USED APPLIANCES ≻

C & C PRE-OWNED APPLIANCES & FURNITURE

2440 Lafayette Rd.
Indianapolis, IN 46222
317/638-4308

Is the only thing stopping you from buying a used appliance the fear that it's going to suddenly fail? C & C offers 60 and 90 day warranties on their merchandise. They sell all major appliances and furniture.

SPEEDWAY APPLIANCES

5240 Crawfordsville Rd.
Speedway, IN 46224
317/244-6048

Microwaves, washers, gas dryers, dishwashers, and ranges are among the list of inventory at Speedway. If you think your old appliance has hope, give them a call. If there's a chance of survival, they'll find it!

TWIN AIR APPLIANCE

3103 English Ave.
Indianapolis, IN 46201
317/685-0439

Imagine, if you will, a world where you don't have to go into debt to buy a new appliance! Twin Air hopes to realize your dream with quality refrigerators, dishwashers, ranges, washers, dryers sold for less.

< PARTS & SERVICE >

A-AFFORDABLE APPLIANCE REPAIR

144 E. Elbert
Indianapolis, IN 46227
317/636-1067

Offering same-day service, A-Affordable Appliance Repair services most makes and models of major appliances. The service charge depends on your zip code, but usually is around $20.00. They offer a conditional guarantee on their work and accept all major credit cards.

A AAA COMPLETE APPLIANCE REPAIR

4835 Southeastern Ave.
Indianapolis, IN 462203

A $20.00 travel and diagnostic charge is applied towards the repair bill. They have several locations throughout the Greater Indianapolis area and offer county wide 24 hour service for Marion County. Call and ask about their three-year conditional warranty and senior discount.
Additional Locations: North 317/844-2918; South 317/788-1816; East 317/352-9702; West 317/244-7205

A BELIEVER APPLIANCE REPAIR CO.

3470 Pleasant Creek Dr.
Indianapolis, IN 46227

Only an $18.00 trip charge within a sixteen mile radius of downtown Indy—and even that charge is applied towards the repair if you choose them to repair your major appliance. They provide prompt, affordable service to all sides of town.
Additional Locations: South/East 317/881-2650
North/West 317/273-0273

APPLIANCE BUSTERS

2332 E. Washington
Indianapolis, IN 46203
317/685-8882

Appliance Busters services all makes and models and the service call is free with repair. Appliance Busters is open seven days a week offering "discounts to all." They pride themselves in their prompt and courteous service.

APPLIANCE PARTS INC.

1734 W. 15th
Indianapolis, IN 46202
317/488-4000

Open since 1930, Appliance Parts Inc. not only stocks genuine replacement parts for major brand appliances, but parts for gas grills as well. You can find parts for your trash compactor, air conditioner, water heater, microwave and about any other appliance that comes to mind.

Additional Locations: 1940 E. Stop 13 Rd. 317/882-2400;
5947 E. 82nd 317/845-1000

BARGAIN APPLIANCE SERVICE

1906 Duke
Indianapolis, IN 46205
317/259-7109

No Service Charge. Bargain Appliance Service is a family owned business that has been servicing the Indianapolis area for over twelve years. They will service any make and model and there is never a service charge—even on evenings or weekends.

BEST APPLIANCE SERVICE

6535 W. Morris
Indianapolis, IN 46241

Best Appliance is available 24 hours, seven days a week and they have one of the lowest service call charges we've seen yet. All work is conditionally guaranteed. They service disposals as well as most makes and models of major appliances.
Additional Locations: North 317/255-3808; South 317/888-2513; East 317/357-1002; West 317/290-1777

MR. FIX-IT SHOP INC.

414 S. Sherman Dr.
Indianapolis, IN 46201
317/356-0880

Since 1961, Mr. Fix-it has been repairing all kinds of small appliances. You may be surprised what can be salvagable—they recently repaired a forty-year old mixer to its original working condition! Don't throw out those broken appliances without bringing them here first.

WEST INDY APPLIANCE PARTS

3837 N. High School Rd.
Indianapolis, IN 46254
317/290-0016

West Indy stocks parts for everything from water heaters to garbage disposals including parts for all major appliances. They offer helpful tips for those who are brave enough to try to repair things themselves, but if by chance you've discovered you are not mechanically inclined, no need to worry, they also sell new appliances.

< SEWING MACHINES >

PLAINFIELD SEW KNIT & VAC

11121 W. Washington
Indianapolis, IN 46231
317/839-9748

Over twenty years of experience in servicing all makes of sewing machines and sergers, makes Plainfield a reliable choice. They are the largest authorized dealer of New Home in Indiana, trade-ins are welcomed and they will give you free machine instructions with the purchase of any new machine. If sergers are more your interest, they also offer training classes for New Home and Bernina Sergers.

SELECT SEWING SERVICE

2802 Lafayette Rd.
Indianapolis, IN 46222
317/926-3483

In a hurry? Select Sewing Service offers two-hour repair service in your home or in their store. With three convenient locations, they're able to keep you sewing without missing a stitch.
Additional Location: 6800 Pendleton Pike 317/545-6176
Glenlake Plaza 317/255-6332

SEWING MACHINE HOSPITAL

4751 Southeastern Ave.
Indianapolis, IN 46203
317/359-4604

Is your sewing machine sick? Call the Sewing Machine Hospital. They have been bringing sewing machines back to life for over 33 years. If your machine is too ill to move, they'll make house calls or send out their ambulance service to pick up and return your machine when it's healthy and ready to go home. If you feel it is your machine's time to meet that big bobbin in the sky, the Sewing Machine Hospital buys machines to insure a proper burial.

≺ VACUUM CLEANERS ≻

A-1 VACUUM CLEANERS SALES & SERVICE

South County Line Mall
Indianapolis, IN 46227
317/888-5839

A-1 Vacuum claims the title of the only factory authorized Hoover sales and service center in Indianapolis. They have been selling and servicing Eureka, Kirby, Rainbow and Royal since 1958. They deal with all major brands, commercial and built-in systems.

BEST VACUUM CLEANERS & JANITORIAL CENTER

622 S. Range Line Rd.
Carmel, IN 46032
317/844-5501

Since 1977, Best Vacuum Cleaners has been offering new and rebuilt vacuums. They service and sell over 30 brands and when you visit their show room, you can choose from over 300 models on display. How's that for cleaning up your act! They accept most major credit cards and offer 90 days same as cash.

DISCOUNT SWEEPER

11337 W. Washington
Indianapolis, IN 46231
317/838-9829

You can trade in a sweeper on its last legs for a new, used, or rebuilt sweeper at Discount Sweeper. But if you just can't part with it, Discount Sweeper will give you a free estimate on repairs.

DISCOUNT VACUUM SALES & SERVICE

9254 Crawfordsville Rd.
Indianapolis, IN 46234
317/297-1944

Discount Vacuum states "We're Sweeping Indianapolis" with low prices on new and used vacuums. If you want to save even more money on your vacuum repair bill visit their do-it-yourself parts department. They sell and service most major name brands such as Hoover, Kirby, Rainbow, and Royal and offer 90 days same as cash. If you're a senior Discount Vacuum offers an additional discount.

SWEEPER WORLD

9042 E. Washington
Indianapolis, IN 46229
317/898-0906

Looking for wholesale prices on vacuums? Sweeper World has new vacuums for sale starting at $99.95 and up. And if that's not good enough, they will beat any competitor's price. Sweeper World offers same-day repair service on all makes and models such as Hoover, Eureka, Kirby, Rainbow and Royal. All major credit cards are accepted.

ART & FRAMES

FRAME DESIGNS

342 Massachusetts Ave.
Indianapolis, IN 46204
317/842-1414

Frame Design has been producing creative custom framing since 1968. They provide free corporate and residential consulting. You can save money on all of your framing needs.
Additional Locations: 11635 Fox Rd. 317/823-4401
118 East 49th St. 317/283-8400

FRAME IT ALL

7821 S. US 31
Indianapolis, IN 46227
317/865-3505

How long ago did you buy that print? And you still haven't framed it? If you take it to Frame It All today you'll get it back...today. Not only do they offer same day service, they also guarantee the quality and the low price. Expect to save about 15% off comparable retail. They also offer a 30% volume discount and a 15% discount to frequent buyers. For your convenience they're open seven days a week and accept major credit cards, checks, and even layaways.
Additional Location: 8435 Castleton Corner Dr. 317/577-2220

FRAME-N-SAVE

9942 E. Washington
Indianapolis, IN 46229
317/897-7676

Frame-N-Save is able to provide custom framing for commercial and residential art work and documents. The do-it-yourselfer can do it for less with their extensive selection of supplies.

FRAMEMAKERS
5660 N. Georgetown Rd.
Indianapolis, IN 46254
317/299-5484

Since 1974 Do-it-yourselfers have been saving money at Framemakers. In fact, so have the rest of us. Whether you plan on making your own frame or letting them do it for you, the savings are noteworthy at Framemakers. One day service is available and Seniors can save even more with their Senior Discount.
Additional Locations: 8607 Allisonville Rd. 317/842-5644
506 S. Range Line Rd., Carmel 317/844-9066

FRAMES PLUS
1675 W. Smith Valley Rd. Suite 1-E
Greenwood, IN 46142
317/887-2380

Save money on corporate art and all of your framing needs. They have over 1,700 mouldings to choose from and can restore your old photographs. Major credit cards are accepted.

MICHAEL'S ARTS & CRAFTS
7639 Shelby St.
Indianapolis, IN 46227
317/881-9277

This store offers extensive craft options. Michael's provides a wide variety of frames and matting at very competitive prices. Also, keep an eye out for their great end-of-season sales. Michaels will beat their competitors' advertised price by 10%.
Additional Locations: 8475 Castleton Corner Dr. 317/842-0577
3619 Commercial Dr. 317/299-9944
10021 E. Washington 317/897-9913

WEIRD LEAF DESIGN CO.

170 N. Madison Ave.
Greenwood, IN 46142
317/882-5887

Looking for that unique gift? No need to look any further. This store has unusual items that are created from nature's own wonders. They also have competitive prices on frames, mats, and prints.

ARTS & CRAFTS

≺ ART SUPPLIES ≻

BATES

5510 E. 82nd
Indianapolis, IN 46250
317/842-8887

If you're a serious art student or just like to create your own priceless wonders, Bates is for you. They carry all major brands of art and drafting supplies. If you run out of acrylics on Sunday afternoon, not to worry; they are open 7 days a week at both of their locations.
Additional Location: 4901 Century Plaza Rd. 317/297-8000

MICHAEL'S ARTS & CRAFTS

7639 Shelby St.
Indianapolis, IN 46227
317/881-9277

This store has it all from A to Z, from artist supplies to zippers. Michael's provides a wide variety of frames and matting at very competitive prices. Also, keep an eye out for their great end-of-season sales. Michael's will beat their competitors' price by 10%!
Additional Locations: 8475 Castleton Corner Dr. 317/842-0577
3619 Commercial Dr. 317/299-9944
10021 E. Washington 317/897-9913

MIZE SUPPLIZE INC.

5440 W. 86th
Indianapolis, IN 46268
317/872-6788

"Be wise, go to Mize" is the advice of this discounter. They have all of your art and graphic materials and they offer a complete line of drawing furniture. All of this and more is offered at commercial and student discounts.

MULTIMEDIA ART MATERIALS

6507 N. College Ave.
Indianapolis, IN 46220
317/255-8552

Need help in deciding which brush to buy? Knowledgeable help can be found at Multimedia Art Materials. Not only can they help you with your decision, but they may also entice you with their student and quantity discounts.

< CRAFT & FLORAL SUPPLIES >

A STITCH IN TIME X-STITCH SUPPLIES

2077 N. Emerson Ave.
Indianapolis, IN 46218
317/357-9909

A Stitch in Time offers thousands of chartbooks, magazines and a complete line of accessories. No request is too hard for them; if they don't have it, they can special order it for you.

ACCENT IN GLASS

5309 W. 10th
Indianapolis, IN 46224
317/241-6103

Did you ever want to learn how to create stained glass? Accent In Glass has the classes to teach would-be glass crafters. They have a full line of tools and supplies, which include over 700 different types of glasses, to get the beginner going. If you're the type who appreciates stained glass, but do not want to create it yourself, then check out their gift items or have them create a custom window for you.

NEEDLE ANTICS

2515 E. Shadeland
Indianapolis, IN 46220
317/253-3500

Learning needle point could provide an easy, economical way to make your own holiday gifts this year and to get you underway, Needle Antics offers classes and supplies to get you started. If you don't have the time, give one of their needle point gifts for the holidays, maybe they'll think you did it yourself.

THE RIBBON OUTLET, INC.

601 Wabash St.
Michigan City, IN 46360
219/874-4953

Thousands and thousands of yards of ribbons to choose from, plain ribbon to the fanciest—this place has it all. They also sell other adornments and notions at their low outlet prices.

< FABRICS & NOTIONS >

CIRCLE FABRIC

3046 N. Shadeland
Indianapolis, IN 46226
317/545-2318

Over 100,000 yards of fabric in stock. Choose from a wide selection that includes vinyl-naugahyde, cottons, prints and much, much, more. Circle Fabric also sells foam cushions that are cut-to-order.

DISCOUNT FABRICS & DRAPERIES

25 E. Court
Franklin, IN 46131
317/736-6515

This store is one city block wide with two selling floors, for a total of 24,000 square feet of retail space. Here you will find the widest selection of fabrics in the state and everything is discounted everyday.

Every imaginable sewing need—upholstery, drapery, bridal and after five, quilt, wool, dress goods, laces, and trims are found here. Discount Fabrics has a wide selection of ready made draperies, tiers, toppers, laces, custom cancellation draperies, and bedspreads. What if they don't have it in stock? Not likely, but if they don't, they also discount special orders. This place knows it's doing its job when the manager sees the store's everyday low price is often lower than other stores' advertised sale prices.

JUST FOR YOU

8914 Southeastern
Indianapolis, IN 46239
317/862-5078

For those of you with a knack for needles, this place is..."Just For You." What better way to display handy work than on beautiful homespun fabrics and cottage laces at this store. All at competitive prices.

LUCAS LITTLE LOVES

432 N. US 31
Whiteland, IN 46184
317/535-0004

Lucas Little Loves specializes in unusual and hard-to-find fabrics. You can expect to find lycra, sequins, knits and much more at Lucas Little Loves. They also offer classes for the sewing impaired.

SOMETHING WONDERFUL

9700 Lakeshore Dr. E.
Indianapolis, IN 46250
317/848-6992

Fine woolens, linens, silk, and lace are among the selection of special occasion fabrics at Something Wonderful. If Something Wonderful doesn't have your item in stock, ask them to special order it. Major credit cards are accepted. Open everyday, except Wednesday and Sunday.

PEALE'S

2629 Shelby St.
Indianapolis, IN 46203
317/784-8914

Where do you go to get fabric for junior's costume for the lead role in *Hamlet*? Peale's. They have a large selection of specialty fabrics and trims, including fringe, rhinestone, feathers, braids and laces. Quality fabrics at competitive prices.

GRIFFON DECORATIVE FABRIC

1408 S. Range Line Rd.
Carmel, IN 46032
317/848-1864

"We'll meet or beat any competitor's prices on identical first-quality fabrics." That's Griffon's promise. Learn how to save money by making your own decorative pillows and other items with their selection of how-to books. A friendly and experienced sales staff will help you make your selection from their full line of first-quality fabrics.

AUTOMOBILES & VEHICLES

≺ ALARMS, STEREOS, & TELEPHONES ≻

MOBILE JAMZZ

4451 N. Keystone Ave.
Indianapolis, IN 46205
317/543-9265

If it's time to replace that old crackling, factory installed radio with your own custom sound system you may want to drop by Mobile Jamzz. They carry the largest selection of custom audio equipment and they will install your audio equipment or their own. Mobile Jamzz also customizes cars from chop tops to pin-striping.

STEREO EXCHANGE

3786 S. East St.
Indianapolis, IN 46227
317/738-5519

If you've been looking for a new stereo but are unable to afford a brand new one, consider pre-owned audio equipment. The Stereo Exchange offers sales and service on major brand name, new and pre-owned equipment, alarms, and accessories.

INDY ELECTRONICS

4374 Madison Ave.
Indianapolis, IN 46227
317/786-4646

Indy Electronics features name brands such as Pioneer, Sony, Panasonic, and Pyle. They'll meet or beat all competitors' prices and do the installation for you. While you're there, check out their great prices on alarms, CBs, and radar detectors.

< BATTERIES >

ACE BATTERY

2166 Bluff Rd.
Indianapolis, IN 46225
317/786-2717

Competitive prices on batteries, terminals, wire and cable. Whether it's for diesels, RV's, the family car or a even a floor scrubber—check out the prices at Ace.

DISCOUNT BATTERY & AUTO ELECTRIC

3002 Madison
Indianapolis, IN 46227
317/783-2288

"Guaranteed lowest prices in Indy" claims Discount Battery. Batteries for just about any vehicles you can think of...autos, trucks, marine, motorcycles, riding-lawn mowers, golf carts, and toy cars are here. Spare the environment—ask about their line of gell cell rechargeable batteries. They offer free installation. Not sure if it's the battery or alternator? They will check it for you for free!
Additional Locations: 3361 Georgetown Rd. 317/299-8888
5104 E. 21st. St. 317-352-1811

INTERSTATE BATTERY

7520 W. Washington
Indianapolis, IN 46231
317/897-9699

You can go "factory direct" on batteries. Interstate Batteries feature quality, dependable batteries at their store Monday through Friday 8:00 a.m. to 5:00 p.m.

< MUFFLERS & BRAKES >

CAR X MUFFLER & BRAKE

6809 W. Washington
Indianapolis, IN 46220
317/247-5527

"Don't worry call the Car-X Man," is the jingle you hear on the radio. Car-X features discount muffler and brake service with a lifetime warranty. On visits to the shop, we have always experienced kind courteous service—they actually take you out in the garage to show and explain what needs to be repaired. The company also shows patriotic spirit by selling Cooper Tires, the only tire that is manufactured in the U.S.

Additional Locations: Several throughout Indiana

MEINEKE MUFFLER

4101 N. Keystone
Indianapolis, IN 46205
317/545-8140

Meineke Muffler offers quality parts with a lifetime guarantee at discount prices. To remove any doubt, they offer free inspections and estimates prior to service. No appointment is needed and you're in and out in 30 minutes or less!

Additional Locations: Several throughout Indiana

RALPH'S MUFFLER

2947 Madison Ave.
Indianapolis, IN 46225
317/781-1516

Bend them, shape them, any way you want...Since 1948, Ralph's Muffler and Brake Shops has been specializing in guaranteed muffler work with no extra service charges. Ralph's encourages customers to compare prices.

Additional Locations: 1250 W. 16th 317/632-9565
6601 E. Washington St. 317/352-9736
4359 N. Keystone Ave. 317/547-4841

< PARTS >

CARBURETOR EXCHANGE

1302 Shelby
Indianapolis, IN 46203
317/634-0365

Carburetor Exchange bills itself as the one-stop shop for all your hard-to-find carburetor parts for foreign or domestic cars. The Carburetor Exchange has been selling and servicing carburetors since 1929.

DISCOUNT HUBCAPS

358 E. Troy Ave.
Indianapolis, IN 46225
317/781-9268

Lost that hubcap on the highway and need a replacement? Discount Hubcaps buys, sells, and trades wheels, wires, hubcaps, and wheel covers. This is the place to find wholesale prices for wheel needs.

FIELDS AUTO PARTS

5388 E. 600 N.
Greenfield, IN 46140
317/326-2271

Fields Auto Parts features a large selection of used engines for around $300. You can get just about everything you need at Fields for just a fraction of the retail cost.

≺ RV SALES, RENTAL & EQUIPMENT ≻

C.E.D. RV CAMPER & VAN RENTALS

3420 S. Post Rd.
Indianapolis, IN 46239
317/862-4411

Want to experience the great outdoors without really roughing it? CED RV offers everything from pop-ups to motor homes with rental plans for any length of time at competitive prices.

MARK'S RV SALES INC.

9702 Pendleton Pike
Indianapolis, IN 46236
317/898-6678

A large selection of motor homes, travel trailers, tent campers, truck campers, tow dollies, and more. Check out their body shop, parts, and service department, too. These things do break down sometimes.

MAYES RV SALES & SERVICE

1099 US 31 S.
Whiteland, IN 46184
317/535-5973
800/535-5973

For over twenty years Mayes RV has offered something for everyone in every phase of RV ownership...sales, parts, service. When you're done with it, they'll sell it on consignment for you. If you're not ready for ownership, call for their low rental rates. They have 10 acres of selection including fold downs, fifth wheels, mini-homes, motor homes, and even camper shells! They also have a complete body shop and are more than happy to do your insurance work.

STOUT'S SOUTHSIDE RV SALES

303 Sheek Rd.
Greenwood, IN 46142
317/881-7670

Over $15 million in inventory, so they tell us. Stout's RV features over 400 units in 20 major brands. "The lowest price on the largest selection of the nation's finest brands," is their promise. They also have propane, a dump station, and a large service department. If you need parts or accessories, Stout's has that too.

≺ SALES ≻

AUTO PURCHASING UNLIMITED

906 N. Delaware
Indianapolis, IN 46202
317/630-1802

Do you absolutely dread negotiations when it's time to buy a new car? Then don't do it. Call Auto Purchasing Unlimited where you can get the low price you're looking for without the sweaty palms that go with it. Simply tell them what make and model you're looking for with what features and they'll do the work—at no fee to you. They have access to the stock of major auto dealers for a small percentage over invoice. The percentage is relatively small because of the volume of business they will give the dealer in the course of a year and the savings are passed on the you. This is a rare find: a discount auto shop.

< TIRES >

TIRE AMERICA

Madison Ave.
Greenwood, IN 46142
317/881-4114

Tire America discounts name tires such as GoodYear, Michelin, BF Goodrich and Dunlop. They will meet or beat any competitors prices 7 days of the week and they'll service you while you wait.
Additional Locations: Several throughout Indiana

TIRE BARN

4000 Georgetown Rd.
Indianapolis, IN 46220
317/328-8473

Tire Barn's motto "Major Brand Quality at Wholesale Prices" says it all. They are open 7 days a week and will beat any advertised price.
Additional Locations: 6221 N. Keystone Ave. 317/257-8473
6415 E 82nd 317/841-8473
789 US 31 N., Greenwood 317/882-8473

BABY NEEDS & TOYS

BABY & KIDS FAIR
State Fair Grounds
317/253-0142

Local merchants of every imaginable baby product get together to display their products and services here. You can find great deals and find out about businesses you probably didn't know existed. There are also 17 large play areas for the children. Held every April at the State Fair Grounds.

BABY RENTALS INC.
123 N. New Jersey
Indianapolis, IN 46204
317/638-3515

Expecting an out-of-town guest? Don't want the baby to sleep in a dresser drawer? Baby Rental's low rental rates allow you to take care of all your temporary baby needs with one stop.

BABY SUPERSTORE
3928 E. 82nd
Indianapolis, IN 46240
317/577-2200

A new parent's dream come true...here you will find everything from newborn clothing to furniture to toddler playhouses. Our recent price check found the regular price on a popular car seat to be $10 lower than the price of a comparable seat at the other "discount" stores.

BURLINGTON COAT FACTORY'S BABY WORLD

7150 E. Washington St.
Indianapolis, IN 46219
317/352-9166

This department in Burlington Coat Factory warrants being a store in itself. Many products you will need for the new little one are found at very competitive prices.

Additional Location: 8275 Broadway, Merrillville 317/736-0636

PATTY CAKES CO.

2960 S. Pennsylvania
Indianapolis, IN 46225
317/784-4321

Your baby's first pair of shoes can be turned into an heirloom-quality keepsake. Bronzing your baby's shoes is convenient and affordable at Patty Cakes.

TOY LIQUIDATORS

11626 N. E. Executive Dr.
Edinburgh, IN 46124
812/526-6838

Toys for every kid and the kid in everyone are found in the discount malls of Indiana. Save up to 70% on popular name brand toys from infants to juniors with something to fit every budget. You can really stretch your Christmas dollar here.

Additional Locations: Horizon Outlet Center, Fremont 219/833-2933
Lighthouse Place Outlet Center, Michigan City 219/872-8882

TOYS 'R US

4575 W. 38th
Indianapolis, IN 46254
317/297-0338

The best buys in toys are here. Right? While they do have a wonderful selection of toys for all ages at competitive prices, they are also nationally recognized for the prices on diapers. If you haven't bought your baby's furniture yet, check out their prices on cribs and mattresses too.

Additional Locations: 1650 E. County Line Rd. 317/882-5838
9251 E. Washington 317/897-0320
8250 Castleton Corner, Fishers 317/841-9334

BEAUTY & SUPPLIES

< SUPPLIES, COSMETICS, & FRAGRANCES >

PRESTIGE FRAGRANCE & COSMETICS

11626 N. E. Executive Dr.
Edinburgh, IN 46124
812/529-9049

Now you can afford to smell like a million bucks. Prestige offers famous maker fragrance at a fraction of department store prices, as much as 70% off.
Additional Locations: Horizon Outlet Center, Fremont
Lighthouse Place, Michigan City 219/872-0977

PERFUMANIA

11626 N. E. Executive Dr.
Edinburgh, IN 46124
812/526-9789

Your probably spending too much on fragrances. Save up to 70% on popular designer fragrance for men and women in the near-to-Indy discount mall off of I65 or in the Northern part of the state.
Additional Locations: Lighthouse Place, Michigan City 219/873-1122

SALLY BEAUTY SUPPLY

7655 S. Shelby
Indianapolis, IN 46227
317/885-1535

Huge selection of beauty products. A variety of copy-cat shampoos and conditioners at savings as much as 50% of name brand products. They also sell nailcare products including nail kits containing everything you need to do your own acrylic nails.
Additional Locations: 5916 Crawfordsville Rd. 317/248-1607
9709 E. Washington 317/897-3399
8370 Castleton Corner 317/578-7748

< WIGS >

AHEAD OF TIMES STYLING

3087 N. High School Rd.
Indianapolis, IN 46224
317/293-4678

Six top professional manufacturers of quality wigs are featured here with styles from short to below the waist in a variety of colors. Ahead of Times keep 20 to 30 wigs in stock and can also place special orders. Prices range from $85 to $125.

DESIGNER'S IMAGE

8402 Harcourt Rd. Suite 104
Indianapolis, IN 46260
317/872-4331

Fifty wigs in stock vary in price from $71 and up. A large selection of styles and colors are available. Stop by or call to make an appointment. Special orders are accepted.

LANA'S BEAUTY SALON & WIGS

4428 E. Michigan
Indianapolis, IN 46201
317/356-4189

Open Tuesday through Saturday, Lana's offers an array of styles and colors, ranging in price from $90 to $160. Special orders are received within three to six days.

ONE BEAUTY SUPPLY

3764 N. Illinois
Indianapolis, IN 46208
317/925-7284

Wares include beauty products, wigs and accessories at competitive prices.

BOATING PRODUCTS

BOATLAND

6225 E. 38th
Indianapolis, IN 46226
317/545-2203

With runabouts, pontoons, and yes, even yachts, Boatland offers a full line of accessories and a knowledgeable service department.

INDIANAPOLIS WATER SPORTS

5025 N. Post Rd.
Indianapolis, IN 46226
317/899-3233

With the average new boat costing the same as an average new mid-size car, you'll do well to go someplace you can trust to make your dream purchase. Indianapolis Water Sports has been family-owned and operated for over 19 years. Six days a week they offer an extensive parts and service department, servicing everything from personal water crafts to larger boats.

JUST ADD WATER

234 S. Franklin
Indianapolis, IN 46219
317/352-1656

Everything from parts, storage and equipment to the boat itself at competitive prices is at this cleverly-named shop. All boats can be demonstrated on their lake, and boats they service are lake-tested.

C.E.D. BOATS

3420 S. Post Rd
Indianapolis, IN 462.
317/862-4411

Open seven days a week, they offer a wide variety of boating products, service, parts, and a full line of accessories. Don't know what to do with your boat this winter? Call and ask about their storage rates.

INDY BOAT SALVAGE

3130 S. Madison Ave.
Indianapolis, IN 46227
317/786-4088

Whether you're buying or selling, Indy Boat Salvage can help save you money. The company has a large array of used parts and boats and buy insurance salvage or just boats off the street.

BOOKS & MAGAZINES

< NEW & USED >

BARNES & NOBLE
3748 E. 82nd
Indianapolis, IN 46240
317/594-7525

Late night studiers looking for Cliff Notes can pick them up at Barnes & Noble. Chances are they'll be open. They're open seven days a week from 7:00 to 11:00. They discount all hard covers by 10%. *New York Times* bestseller picks are discounted at 30%, and 20% is offered on *New York Times* bestseller paper backs.

BOOK WAREHOUSE
11626 N. E. Executive Dr.
Edinburgh, IN 46124
812/526-9860

Books for everyone is the offering of this mall outlet store, all at deep savings. A large selection of everything from children's books to self-help books. A good portion of their stock is remainders, but they're the same books you've seen recently at the local book store. Save 50% to 90%.
Additional Location: Horizon Outlet Center, Fremont 317/833-6720

BOOKLAND
8275 Broadway
Merrillville, IN 46410
219/769-2982

Books, Books, Books. Over 100,000 to be exact. All at savings up to 90% from the publisher's list price.

BORDERS BOOK SHOP

5612 Castleton Corner Ln.
Indianapolis, IN 46250
317/849-8660

Borders has literally hundreds of thousands of titles per store. And if it's a hard cover on the *New York Times* bestseller list it will be discounted by 30%.

INDIANA NEWS CO.

14 W. Maryland
Indianapolis, IN 46225
317/636-7680

Out-of-state papers? Look no farther. At Indiana News you can get the *Chicago Tribune* or *Village Voice*—all for far less than it would cost to fly there and get it yourself. Most Sunday papers will come in the following Monday.

THOMAS BOOKS

7421 US 31 S
Indianapolis, IN 46227
317/865-2200

Tables and tables full of marked-down books are in this Southside shop. They often offer additional savings with the purchase of five of more discounted books over $4.95. We recently found a popular coffee table book that no one else in town had in stock.

≺ USED ≻

BLUE RIVER BOOKS

20 E. Maryland
Indianapolis, IN 46204
317/237-0323

New and used books on a variety of subjects including history and Indiana authors. Mostly hardbacks.

BROAD RIPPLE BOOKSHOP

6407 Ferguson St.
Indianapolis, IN 46220
317/259-1980

Used paperbacks and hard-cover books in all sorts of subjects are available where the ducks quack. Bring in your used paperbacks and they will give credit towards your purchase. Drop off your hard covers and they will determine the value to buy.

FOUNTAIN OF MYSTERY BOOKS

1119 Prospect
Indianapolis, IN 46203
317/635-2583

The largest mystery store in Central Indiana! Mostly used hardback and paperback mystery books are found here, but you will also see hardback and paperback science-fiction, paperback westerns, and limited selection of non-fiction. In all, about 30,000 books. Save 10% when you spend $10.00, 15% for $25.00, and 20% for $50.00. Bookdealers get a 20% discount. The owner recently visited England and Scotland where she purchased over 500 new and used mysteries (sorry, these aren't discounted) to add to the vast selection. Fountain of Mystery Books accepts Mastercard, Visa and checks and is open Tuesday through Saturday.

FRIENDS OF THE LIBRARY BOOK SALE

2450 N. Meridian.
Indianapolis, IN 462
317/269-1772

Held six times a year for the general public, this enormous benefit sale features used library books sold at really steep discounts. For a membership fee of $15 you can become a Friend of the Library and go to the sneak preview the night before the sale to get first pick on these great bargains.

HALF PRICE BOOKS RECORDS & MAGAZINES

844 N. US 31
Greenwood, IN 46142
317/889-1076

A bookworm's paradise, this store chain has come a long way since its humble beginnings in a converted laundromat in Dallas, Texas way back in 1972. Now they're the largest new and used bookstore chain in the nation! It's obvious why when you look at their policies. Trained buyers examine used books and pay cash depending on their condition and salability. They offer a selection of more than 100,000 books. You will also find a good selection of cassettes, LPs, CDs, videos and comics. On average you will save 50% of publisher's list price, but you can usually find quite a few for as much as 80% off regular retail. Some items are excluded, like collectibles, but not many. Some of their unique policies are: a kids' frequent reading club, a 10% discount for teachers and librarians, gift certificates good at locations throughout the country, donations to non-profit organizations, and "Books By The Yard" for decorating needs. Their recycling efforts have saved approximately 300,000 trees! You'll be amazed at their selection and your savings.

Additional Locations: 1551 W. 86th 317/824-9002
8316 Castleton Corner Dr. 317/577-0410

MURDER & MAYHEM

6411 Carrollton Ave.
Indianapolis, IN 46220
317/254-8273

Halloween happens every day here. It's a Broad Ripple mystery specialty store. You'll also find horror, dark suspense, and children's mysteries.

THE PAPERBACK SHACK & COMICS INC.

1752 E. 116th
Carmel, IN 46032
317/844-4232

Turn off the TV and pick up a good book. The Paperback Shack & Comics Inc. have all the ingredients for a rainy Sunday afternoon. Stop buy and pick up several of your favorite paperbacks without parting from many of your greenbacks.

THE BOOK RACK

3780 S. East St.
Indianapolis, IN 46227
317/783-2473

What do you do with all your paperbacks after you've read them? You could be getting cash at the Book Rack. They will give you credit toward the purchase of more books if you wish.
Additional Locations: 6144 W. 25th 317/297-8968
8013 E. Washington 317/897-2173
County Line Mall 317/783-2473

THE TRADING LIBRARY

1912 Broad Ripple Ave.
Indianapolis, IN 46220
317/255-5852

Bring in your old paperbacks and get credit toward the purchase of more at this used paperback book store.

BUILDING & REMODELING

≺ AIR CONDITIONING & HEATING ≻

AFFORDABLE SERVICE & CONSTRUCTION

2538 S. Meridian
Indianapolis, IN 46225
317/784-2023

Affordable offers free estimates and 24-hour emergency service at no extra charge. They have over 30 years experience, and they accept Visa and Mastercard.

PAUL E. SMITH CO., INC.

8171 W. 10th
Indianapolis, IN 46214
317/271-2222

"Solutions you can rely on" is this store's motto. Well, they probably didn't grow to four stores by leaving their customers out in the cold. They're open 24 hours a day, 365 days a year and have service that can't be beat. They don't consider your unit fixed until it has worked perfectly for six months. If it fails under their guarantee, they'll fix it for free. Plus, they don't charge more for extra labor and hard-to-find parts. If your unit is old, don't despair; they also stock parts for units over 10 years old.

Additional Locations: North 317/845-4455
South 317/882-6600
East 317/5451600

< BRICKS, BLOCKS, & MASONRY >

QUALITY STONE

St. Rd. 38 East
Noblesville, IN 46060
317/773-5597

Stone from 37 states delivered to wherever you want. Quality Stone has a complete selection including patio, walk, veneer, flag, and landscaping stones and more.

STONE CENTER OF INDIANA

5272 E. 65th St.
Indianapolis, IN 46220
317/849-9100
800/300-3197

Fireplace stone, used brick, flagstone, sand retaining stones, and pebbles are only a small sample of what you will find at the Stone Center. Their friendly staff is more than happy to give advice and consultation for your project as part of their service—for no extra charge. They also have statuary for the finishing touches on your landscape.

SCHUSTER'S BLOCK, INC.

901 E. Troy Ave.
Indianapolis, IN 46203
317/787-3201

Schuster's Block, Inc. has been serving Central Indiana since 1918 with block and brick. They have a large inventory of face brick, concrete and clay pavers, patio brick and more. Their display area can help you determine your needs. They're always open Monday through Friday; Saturday hours are seasonal.

< CABINETS & COUNTERTOPS >

CABINET FACTORY OUTLETS

8530 E. 33rd
Indianapolis, IN 46226
317/897-5439

You'll find factory-direct cabinets for a fraction of the regular retail price at Cabinet Factory Outlet. You can choose from several styles of discontinued and surplus cabinets.

DISCOUNT CABINET INC.

5601 E. 38th
Indianapolis, IN 46218
317/545-2104

Discount Cabinet, Inc. offers a large selection of residential and commercial cabinets. They'll install, or you can save even more by doing it yourself. In addition to cabinets, they'll also reduce prices on floor coverings, formica tops, appliances, and window coverings.

KITCHENLAND

3524 N. Shadeland
Indianapolis, IN 46226
317/545-1520

Kitchenland buys direct from the factory and pass the savings on to you. Their staff can help you lay out and plan your dream kitchen Monday through Saturday.

< DOORS, WINDOWS, & MIRRORS >

AMERIVINYL WHOLESALE

6601 E. 10th St.
Indianapolis, IN 46214
317/897-3668

Top quality windows, doors, and siding are featured here at great discounts. Amerivinyl Wholesale offers free estimates and customer satisfaction is guaranteed.

BEE WINDOW INC.

1002 E. 52nd St.
Indianapolis, IN 46208
317/283-8522

Their motto is "We manufacture—you save." Bee claims..."the strongest warranty in the business." You will probably not only save money by comparison to comparable retail, but also in reduced energy bills.

BEVELED GLASS & LIGHTING DESIGNS

3185 N. Shadeland
Indianapolis, IN 46226
317/547-5256

Beveled Glass & Lighting Designs features a 5,000 square foot showroom. Choose from a variety of designs in their complete lines for less than comparable retail. If you're having trouble deciding which lights and doors will look good with your home, ask to schedule an appointment with one of their lighting consultants. Flexible appointment hours are available.

HOME LUMBER & SUPPLY CO.

901 E. New York
Indianapolis, IN 46202
317/637-4561

Since 1920 this family-owned-and-operated business has been locating hard-to-find building products for contractors and the do-it-yourselfer. We were looking for composite siding and Home Lumber & Supply Co. had it, with the design we needed, in stock.

INDOORS OUTDOORS

4800 N. Keystone Ave.
Indianapolis, IN 46205
317/255-4140

Indoors Outdoors sells quality window guards and security doors at very competitive prices, offering free in-home estimates. Financing is available.

WHOLESALE HARDWOOD INTERIORS INC. OF INDIANAPOLIS

4305 W. 96th
Indianapolis, IN 46268
317/872-3938

Chair rail for your dining room, crown molding for the game room, or a whole house full of trim, quality woodwork is available at affordable prices here.

< ELECTRICAL & PLUMBING >

ECONOMY PLUMBING

625 N. Capitol Ave.
Indianapolis, IN 46204
317/264-2240

Serving Central Indiana for over 60 years, Economy claims it will work within your budget to provide you with quality stock and custom cabinets for kitchen and bath. We recently found a marble shell-shaped sink top for $40.00. They stock thousands of parts and are happy to answer any questions. They're open Monday through Saturday, so homeowners can shop on weekends for their convenience.

KIRBY RISK SUPPLY CO.

1440 W. 16th
Indianapolis, IN 46202
317/687-0015

Featuring a complete stock of electrical supplies and equipment, Kirby caters to residential, commercial, and even industrial markets.

< FENCING >

AMSTEEL

5151 W. 10th
Indianapolis, IN 46202
317/241-2804

Tired of wondering where Rover has wandered to? Just put up a fence. Amsteel sells chainlink, split rail, picket, cape cod and more. With over 30 years experience, Amsteel is dedicated to saving their customers money.

FOUR SQUARE FENCE CO.

200 E. Main St.
Greenwood, IN 46142
317/888-7435

If a fence is in your future Four Square can provide you with a free, no obligation estimate and help you determine your needs. Save money by installing it yourself, or, if you rather, let them do—their rates are very affordable.

J & W FENCE SUPPLY

1736 W. Epler Ave.
Indianapolis, IN 46217
317/783-4111
800/222-7794

With over three decades of service to Indianapolis, J & W believes they continue to provide their customers with great value. In addition to selling a vast array of fencing, they also offer dog kennels, picnic tables, gazebo kits, lawn furniture, railroad ties, lattice, and over 36 variations of playground equipment. Visa and Mastercard are accepted and 90 days same as cash is offered. On their two-acre display area a helpful staff will help you choose the product that best fits your needs.

< FIREPLACES >

POOL CITY

940 Fry Rd.
Greenwood, IN 46142
317/888-3933

They sell more than just pools and pool supplies here. Pool City has a large selection of gas and wood fireplaces, gas logs, and a complete line of hearth accessories. Free estimates for running gas lines are available. They also have all of the chemicals you could possibly need, accessories, and a variety of sizes and styles of pools and hot tubs, all at competitive prices.
Additional Location: 3826 Georgetown Rd. 317/297-3612

WATSON'S

11801 Pendleton Pike
Oaklandon, IN 46236
317/823-4448

Featuring brands such as Hargrove, Peterson, Valor, Appalachian and others, Watson's offers a the selection of ventless fireplaces, gas inserts and accessories. Maybe instead of a fireplace, you're looking for a pool or hot tub? With extensive selection, their hot tub packages start just under $2,000, and they have a large service department to service what they sell.

< FLOORING >

BENNY'S CARPET

8140 Pendently Pike
Indianapolis, IN 46226
317/545-4400

Everyday savings of 20 to 30% on not just your everyday flooring. Benny's has top-quality flooring including carpeting, vinyl, ceramic tile and more—for less. They have over 500 carpet remnants and about 75 vinyl remnants. In addition to their remnants, they also carry 30 to 50 full rolls of carpet and vinyl and stock six different types of paddings. Eight out of ten customers can obtain carpet, pad, and labor all in one day. No waiting or ordering. The company stands behind what they sell. Layaways and in-store financing are available and they also accept Visa and Mastercard. Additional discounts are given if you're purchasing for the whole house or if you're an Interior Designer. If you don't know exactly how much you need, Benny's provides a professional measurer to estimate your needs so you don't waste any or come up too short.

BROTHERS FLOOR COVERINGS

6229 Carrollton Ave.
Indianapolis, IN 46220
317/251-0350

In business since1952, Brothers offers competitive prices on major brands of quality flooring with hundreds of samples to choose from, whether you're looking for herringbone or parquet hardwood floors or custom borders.

THE CARPET BARN

4016 S. Meridian
Indianapolis, IN 46217
317/787-5738

Major brands at steep discounts. The Carpet Barn offers free estimates. Installation is also available.

CARPET VALUES INC.

3817 S. East St.
Indianapolis, IN 46227

Save 30 to 70% on popular brands of carpet. A large assortment of colors and styles are available for your choosing. Layaways and in-store financing are available and major credit cards are accepted.

GRAHAM'S CARPET

2525 25th St.
Columbus, IN 47201
812/372-3311

Margins are a lot lower at Graham's than at other shops, so you will be able to save on carpeting, vinyl flooring, hardwood, luxury vinyl, tile and even remnants. Their friendly staff will help you with any questions you may have and aid you in making your selection. They are an exclusive TrustMark dealer.

INDIANA WOOD FLOORS INC.

5508 Elmwood Ave. Suite 417
Indianapolis, IN 46203
317/787-4149

"We buy direct from the mills and you save." All of the top manufacturing names in hardwood flooring should be available when you visit. They also sell supplies, including everything you need to do it yourself. Indiana Wood Floors has been family-owned and operated since 1937.

MEES TILE & MARBLE INC.

3401 N. Shadeland
Indianapolis, IN 46226
317/546-9595

A large inventory of marble, slate, quarry, ceramic and more is available, and you may save even more money on discontinued styles and special buys. They've been importing and distributing for over 50 years.

REMNANT FACTORY

8801 Crawfordsville Rd.
Indianapolis, IN 46234
317/299-8921

At the Remnant Factory you can save money on pieces of carpet that have already been cut from the roll. They have a large selection of colors and styles to choose from.

TILE MART

4708 Century Plaza Rd.
Indianapolis, IN 46254
317/329-0400

Over two million square feet of ceramic tile are in stock at Tile Mart. They advertise prices at or below wholesale. In addition to ceramic floor and wall tile they also sell no-wax vinyl, professional hardwood floors and supplies. Their inventory is from bankrupt inventories, overruns, closeouts and direct from the manufacturer.

≺ HOME IMPROVEMENTS ≻

MAJESTIC HOME IMPROVEMENT CO., INC.

2806 E. Michigan
Indianapolis, IN 46201
317/632-2302

Since 1950 Majestic Home Improvement has been offering savings on roofing, siding, window and door replacement, and other home improvement needs. Give them a call for an estimate. They proudly refer to their reputation for doing quality work and standing behind what they do. Those over 65 can save even more with their Senior Discount.

≺ ONE-STOP HARDWARE STORES ≻

AMERICAN HARDWARE & SUPPLY CO.

1018 Virginia Ave.
Indianapolis, IN 46203
317/637-0294

American Hardware has a complete line of plumbing supplies and hardware at competitive prices.

BUILDER'S SQUARE

3695 Commercial Dr.
Indianapolis, IN 46222
317/291-3468

Lumber, lighting, wall coverings, lawn and patio items, hardware and more are shown at discount prices under one roof.
Additional Locations: 602 N. Shortridge Rd. 317/356-3012
8040 US 31 South 317/885-1600

MENARD'S
6450 Gateway Dr.
Indianapolis, IN 46254
317/297-7458

Thousands and thousands of square feet of building supplies and household wares make this a favorite Indy do-it-yourself center.
Additional Locations: 6800 Pendleton Pike 317/549-2696
7140 S. Emerson 317/580-9400

≺ TOOLS ≻

BLACK & DECKER
11626 N. E. Executive Dr.
Edinburgh, IN 46124
812/526-8321

Save up to 35% on tools, small appliance, hardware and more on this nationally famous brand. They're open seven days a week at the Horizon Outlet Center and accept major credit cards.

TOOL WAREHOUSE
11626 N. E. Executive Dr.
Edinburgh, IN 46124
812/526-5298
Outlet prices on tools for the home, garage, workshop and outdoors.

— *TOOL RENTAL* —

BUSARD RENTS
1330 Main St.
Speedway, IN 46224
317/241-2543

Tile cutters, automotive tools, log splitters, sanders, lawn mowers, tillers and more can be rented at this Speedway location.

JACK'S TOOL RENTAL

861 N. Range Line Rd
Carmel, IN 46032
317/846-0651

"Choose from one of Indy's largest inventories of tool and equipment. Perfect for everyone from the contractor to the do-it-yourselfer" so they say. Renting is a satisfactory answer for millions of Americans with small jobs to do.
Additional Locations: Fishers, IN 317/595-0651; 800/2276-8665
Downtown Indianapolis 317/926-0651

THE TOOL SHED

2705 E. Washington
Indianapolis, IN 46201
317/636-1818

Over three acres of tools and equipment. Air-mailers, concrete equipment, lawn & garden tools, post hole diggers, and welding equipment are just some of the equipment they have available for rental. Weekend renting adds to your savings. They pride themselves in clean, dependable equipment. Major credit cards are accepted.

CARDS & GIFTS

CARD FACTORY

601 Wabash St.
Michigan City, IN 46360
219/879-1099

A wide selection of cards, wrapping paper and novelty gifts at savings up to 50%—even more on clearance items.

DIVERSIONS *

9546 Allisonville Rd. Suite 134
Indianapolis, IN 46250
317/578-3336

Diversions has gifts for every age, everything from a large selection of unique small toys for children to heirloom quality collectibles. Want to jazz up the gift a bit? Custom made gift baskets and balloon wrapping are available—and affordable. They also sell greeting cards, gourmet coffees and specialty chocolates. Since 1990, they have been providing one-stop gift shopping on the North and South sides of town. They're open seven days a week and accept major credit cards. Be sure to see their coupon in the back for additional savings.
Additional Location:
1675 W. Smith Valley Rd., Greenwood 317/865-9014

FACTORY CARD OUTLET

5926 Crawfordsville Rd.
Indianapolis, IN 46224
317/388-9277

Their trademark is a huge selection of quality greeting cards at an unbelievably low everyday price of 39¢. They usually display a wide selection in gift wrap, party supplies, giftware and seasonal goods. Savings average 20 to 90%. Balloon bouquets and custom made centerpieces add to the party atmosphere. A large selection of helium

filled balloons are under 60¢ and Mylar balloons are only $1.69. Seniors receive 10% of their purchases all day on Wednesday.
Additional Locations: Several throughout Indiana

KRIEG BROS. CATHOLIC SUPPLY HOUSE
119 S. Meridian
Indianapolis, IN 46225
317/638-3416

They can offer suggestions for confirmations, weddings or any other occasion.

THE PAPER FACTORY
5736 Crawfordsville Rd.
Speedway, IN 46224
317/241-7554

The Paper Factory has a complete line of party goods for everything from weddings to luaus. They work at offering prices that are the "lowest around." They sell two-sheet flat wrapping paper for $2.00. They also wind down large rolls of gift wrap into smaller rolls to pass savings on to their customers. There are no cardboard cores—it's all gift wrap. They specialize in balloon arrangements and centerpieces for special occasions. Savings are from 10 to 50%. Seniors get 10% on purchases of $5.00 or more on Wednesday. A Frequent Party Club Card and Rewind Club Card can also save frequent buyers money. Case discounts are available and volume discounts are given to those with tax exempt ID numbers.
Additional Locations:
Horizon Outlet Center, Edinburgh 812/526-5096
5534 Grape Rd., Mishawaka 219/277-2763
Horizon Outlet Center, Fremont 219833-6424
Lighthouse Place, Michigan City 219/874-8447

TASTY'S GIFT FACTORY

4014 W. 96th
Indianapolis, IN 46268
317/726-0000

A large selection of gifts, including novelty. Items can be arranged in a gift basket. Check out a current copy of *Nuvo*; they usually have a gift basket special advertised.

CLEANING & STORAGE

< BOXES >

ALLIED BOX CO.

2525 N. Shadeland Ave. Suite E-41
Indianapolis, IN 46219
317/352-0083

If you need a box for a special need or just to move—they have a box for you. Allied Box Co. buys and sells over run, surplus, and used boxes in addition to their already large inventory of new boxes. They also carry all supplies necessary for shipping and moving.

BOXES N' MORE

2312 E. County Line Rd.
Indianapolis, IN 46227
317/881-5588

Wholesale and retail boxes in a variety of sizes. Buy a bunch and save a lot, they offer a quantity discount and will help you determine what size you need. Gift wrapping is also available.

CAPITOL CITY CONTAINER CORP.

5005 W. 81st
Indianapolis, IN 46268
317/875-0290
800/233-5145

For all your packaging needs, Capitol City Container Corp. is there for you. They carry a large selection of stock and custom boxes. Let them box all of your cares away.

≺ CLEANING SERVICES ≻

SPIFFY MAID

317/882-5050

This is a classic American rags-to-riches story. Years ago a young girl in Atlanta was orphaned; at the orphanage she learned the wonderful art of thorough cleaning. When she was old enough to leave the orphanage she supported herself with her one-woman cleaning service. Through hard work and perseverance that one-woman operation has turned into a chain of 700. They're known nation-wide for their quality work and affordable prices. Even with such a large business, she hasn't rested on her laurels; to this day she is still active in the daily operations. Whether you're too busy to clean your house or just aren't able to, call one of their locations for an estimate. It's also a great idea for your vacation lake home. Who wants to drive all the way there and then have to spend the next few hours cleaning before you can relax? Spiffy will send someone ahead of you, so you can enjoy your time away. They stand behind their work 100% and you will be amazed how affordable it can be.

Additional locations: Northeast 317/475-1111, South 317/882-5050, Northwest 317/329-9999

PURCELL'S CLEANING

317/856-6822

Aaagh! Is time for spring cleaning again? Didn't you just do that? Let somebody else do it for you. Purcell's has all kinds of cleaning packages available. Whether you need it weekly, biweekly, monthly, or just once a year, give them a call for a free estimate. They'll ask you a few questions about the size and condition of your home. They pride themselves in quality work. It doesn't matter if it's just the general cleaning you need or deep down "yuk" removal, they can give you an estimate based on exactly what you need.

CLOTHING & ACCESSORIES

≺ ACCESSORIES ≻

BURNHAM GLOVE
1602 Tennessee St.
Michigan City, IN 46360
219/874-5205

Since 1901, Burnham has been keepin' 'em warm! Gloves of every imaginable kind, including dress gloves for adults and children are featured at savings from 33.3% to 75% below retail.

FINCORP
173 E. Broadway St.
Greenwood, IN 46142
317/881-8242

Sports logo apparel in a variety of styles and colors for men, women and children. Prices are less than clearance at department stores.

LEATHER LOFT
11626 N. E. Executive Dr.
Edinburgh, IN 46124
812/526-2366

South on I65 at the Horizon Outlet Center, Edinburgh. You'll find designer purses, luggage, briefcases, and accessories at low prices. Yes! They also have leather jackets.

LEATHER MANOR
601 Wabash St.
Michigan City, IN 46360
219/879-6916

Saving up to 70% on popular name brand leather goods. A large selection of hand bags, brief cases, and luggage.
Additional Location: Horizon Outlet Center, Fremont 219/833-2588

STONE MOUNTAIN HANDBAGS

11626 N. E. Executive Dr.
Edinburgh, IN 46124
812/526-8110

What the name doesn't mention is the savings, up to 70% you'll get on these first quality items at two outlet malls in Indiana.
Additional Location: Lighthouse Place, Michigan City 219/873-0048

SWANK

11626 N. E. Executive Dr.
Edinburgh, IN 46124
812/526-2800

Accessories Galore! Jewelry, belts, handbags, perfumes, and even gift items. Expect to save 40% to 70%.

TOTES/SUNGLASS WORLD

601 Wabash St.
Michigan City, IN 46360
219/874-1350

We're guessing the "totes" portion of the name is attributed to their selection of...you know what. A large selection of umbrellas, rubber boots, rain coats, and folding lugging. Not all locations have the Sunglass World section.
Additional Location: Horizon Outlet Center, Fremont 219/833-2388

WALLET WORKS

601 Wabash St.
Michigan City, IN 46360
219/872-4985

Savings of 20% to 75% off retail on items like wallets, handbags, briefcases, luggage, and accessories. Their stock is first-quality and direct from the manufacturer.

≺ ACTIVE WEAR ≻

BON WORTH

11626 N. E. Executive Dr.
Edinburgh, IN 46124
812/526-8386

A large selection of misses and ladies Bon Worth clothing at saving between 30% to 60%. Save up to 90% on some clearance items.

LOGO 7 OUTLET STORE

3203 N. Shadeland
Indianapolis, IN 46226
317/895-7005

Open seven days a week, Logo 7 features NFL, NBA, baseball, and college sportswear at dramatic savings from department store prices.

THE SWEATSHIRT CO.

11626 N. E. Executive Dr.
Edinburgh, IN 46124
812/526-0545

Sweatshirts and active wear for absolutely everyone in the family. A large selection of colors and styles ranging from children to ladies plus sizes to men's big and tall.

WHOLESALE T-SHIRT SUPPLY

1352 N. Illinois
Indianapolis, IN 46202
317/634-4423

For those of you who like to add your own touch to your clothes, you'll find plain T-Shirts and sweatshirts for the whole family at Wholesale T-Shirt. They also sell printable towels, boxer shorts, dorm shirts, caps and much more all at discounted prices.

≺ BRIDAL & FORMAL ≻

BRIDAL OUTLET

6348 E. 82nd St.
Indianapolis, IN 46250
317/842-8868

No matter what the formal occasion, you can expect substantial savings over the usual break-the-bank bridal price tags at Bridal Outlet. A variety of bridal, pageant and formal wear is in stock. They also carry full figure gowns—in stock!

BRIDE & GROOM BRIDAL SHOP

7900 Madison Ave.
Indianapolis, IN 46227
317/881-0099

We recently found a gown here for half the price it was in the fancy shops. They have a wide selection of gowns and bridesmaids dresses to choose from, all at outlet prices. Why spend the family savings when you don't have to?

BRIDE'S ETC.

8611 N. Michigan Rd.
Indianapolis, IN 46268
317/875-5557

There isn't much sense in spending a fortune on something you'll only need once. This shop allows you to rent your gown and brides maid dresses. If you prefer to buy your own gown, you can also purchase it here at competitive prices.

DIANA'S BRIDAL BOUTIQUE

8025 E. Washington
Indianapolis, IN 46219
317/898-5171

Did you see the perfect dress in a magazine? Check with Diana's to see if she can stitch it from a pattern—you'll save! From size 4 to 32. The savings are bliss, spend 'em on caviar at the reception. They also offer expert alterations.

DISCOUNT BRIDAL SERVICE
5528 E. Fall Creek Pkwy. N. Dr.
Indianapolis, IN 46226
317/545-5444

Save on everything you need for your wedding. Call for an appointment.

HE-RO GROUP
601 Wabash St.
Michigan City, IN 46360
219/879-4237

"Wow!" That was our first impression when we visited this store at Lighthouse Place. More beaded and finely detailed dresses than we've ever seen in one place. Save 30 to 60% on evening and special occasion wear by Black Tie, Niteline and others. The "others" are very recognizable designer labels that we aren't allowed to mention by name. They accept all major credit cards and checks.

MARY'S BRIDAL BARGAINS
5953 E. 82nd St.
Indianapolis, IN 46250
317/842-0972

Save a least 25% off retail. Mary's has a large selection of wedding gowns, veils, and bridesmaids dresses in stock. For one-stop shopping, mothers' dresses and tuxes also available. Open seven days a week.

— *RENTALS* —

TOP HAT TUXEDOS
938 E. Georgia St.
Indianapolis, IN 46202
317/639-6060

Whether you need to rent or buy, this is the place to go to save 10 to 30%. Top Hat offers competitive rates on rentals and a variety of specials. For example, the groom's tux rental is free with five paid rentals. They also sell discontinued lines at the Georgia St. location at huge savings.
Additional Locations: 5850 E. 82nd 317/842-4090
Washington Square 317/899-4220
Lafayette Square 317/293-6477
Greenwood Park 317/888-8393
4614 Coldwater Rd., Ft. Wayne 219/484-1022

≺ FAMILY APPAREL ≻

BENNETON
601 Wabash St.
Michigan City, IN 46360
219/874-5827

Clothes from everywhere for juniors, women and men in all of the season's most popular styles for less than "mall" prices. They accept most major credit cards.

BUGLE BOY
11626 N. E. Executive Dr.
Edinburgh, IN 46124
812/526-0771

Genuine Bugle Boy clothing at a fraction of the cost! This factory-owned store means saving up to 60% on men, women, and juniors.
Additional Locations: Horizon Outlet Center, Fremont 219/833-6720
Lighthouse Place, Michigan City 219/874-5667

BURLINGTON COAT FACTORY

7150 E. Washington St.
Indianapolis, IN 46219
317/352-9166

Great savings on just about everything, for everybody in the family. Popular brands in current styles, for less money.
Additional Location: 8275 Broadway, Merrillville 219/736-0636

CASH BARGAIN CENTER

2711 Madison Ave.
Indianapolis, IN 46225
317/783-4606

Cash Bargain Center offers family clothing at factory-outlet prices or lower! Founded in 1968 by a family that has been retailing in Indianapolis since 1897, Cash Bargain Center offers famous brands such as Levi, Limited, Polo, Buster Brown, and more. In addition to first-quality merchandise, whopping savings can be found in the slight-irregulars and seconds that are sometimes available in the branded merchandise. Savings average 20 to 60%. All three locations are usually "busting at the seams" with lots of merchandise to choose from. Although the name may imply otherwise, checks and charge cards are also welcome here.
Additional Location: 25th & Sherman Dr. 317/546-4606
71st & Michigan Rd. 317/293-5995

CHAMPION HANES

11626 N. E. Executive Dr.
Edinburgh, IN 46124
812/526-2592

From top to bottom, a champion of savings on men and women's apparel. A large selection of colors and styles of active wear.
Additional Location: Lighthouse Place, Michigan City 219/872-9254

EAGLE'S EYE

601 Wabash St.
Michigan City, IN 46360
219/879-6510

First-Quality and slightly irregular active wear and career wear for ladies. Fashion for 40% of 60% less.

IZOD FACTORY STORE

11626 N. E. Executive Dr.
Edinburgh, IN 46124
219/872-8695

Save 30% to 50% off manufacturer's suggested retail and still enjoy that great Izod fit. In addition to the title brands, you will also find Gant, Eagle, and Palm Beach. men's and women's apparel and accessories, and even a selection for children. Ladies, you'll even save on Monet and Trifari jewelry.
Additional Locations: Horizon Outlet Center, Fremont 219/833-2634
1203 Lighthouse Place, Michigan City 219/833-2634

LEVI'S OUTLET BY DESIGNS

11626 N. E. Executive Dr.
Edinburgh, IN 46124
812/526-9644

Why wait for a sale? Here you will find everyday low prices on Levi Apparel at or below department store sale prices. They offer a complete selection of Levi 's in a variety of styles.

MACY'S CLOSE OUT

8141 Pendleton Pike
Indianapolis, IN 46226
317/897-5018

Racks and racks jam-packed with famous maker labels in men's, women's and juniors are at Macy's. Most prices start at about 50% of the original retail. They also have a good sized shoe department and frequent sales.

THE MANUFACTURER'S OUTLET
7803 E. Washington
Indianapolis, IN 46219
317/352-0780

All kinds of labels have been brought together here under one roof, with a diverse selection of apparel at big savings.

OILILY
601 Wabash St.
Michigan City, IN 46360
219/872-3577

A very unique selection of clothing, bright colors and design make this store a visual treat.

POLO/RALPH LAUREN
601 Wabash St.
Michigan City, IN 46360
219/874-9442

Save up to 50% on men, women and boys apparel. (Sorry Girls.) They also offer some home furnishings and accessories—and, even fragrances.
Additional Locations: Horizon Outlet Center, Fremont 219/833-6255

SIDE OUT
601 Wabash St.
Michigan City, IN 46360
219/879-1446

Quality apparel for, on average, 30% less than regular retail with a large selection of casual wear and separates in a variety of sizes. Some clearance reductions are made early in the season, so you can save money on very contemporary styles. They accept major credit cards.

SOCKS GALORE
11626 N. E. Executive Dr.
Edinburgh, IN 46124
812/5262422

Thousands and thousands and thousands of socks. In every imaginable colors, from fashion socks to sweat socks, and you can get them up to 80% off from what you spend at a department store for the same name brands.
Additional Locations: Lighthouse Place, Michigan City 219/879-2244
Horizon Outlet Centers, Fremont 219/833-2590

T.J. MAXX
5415 E. 82nd
Indianapolis, IN 46250
317/842-4727

From Lingerie to infant wear, the only thing missing is maternity. A constantly changing inventory of popular name brand apparel and accessories. Their housewares department is one of our favorite with a unique collection of dishes, picture frames, decorating item and more.
Additional Locations: 8800 US 31 S. 317/881-3957
Cherry Tree Shopping Center 317/897-5819
3733 Commercial Dr. 317/293-1144

≺ FURS & LEATHER GARMENTS ≻

DAY FURS
1361 S. Rangeline Rd.
Carmel, IN 46032
317/844-8733

Day Furs features men's and ladies' wear in award-winning designs. Perhaps you already have a nice fur that just needs doctoring a bit...Day Furs offers skilful styling and repair. Temperature-controlled storage is also available.

VINCENT FURS

S. R. 67
Mooresville, IN 46
317/831-5400

Vincent's stands by the customer after the sale. They offer such valued services as storage, cleaning and even repair. Over 1,000 fur and leather coats to choose from. Watch for their "Once a Year Sale" and save 15 to 50%.

< INFANT'S & CHILDREN'S APPAREL >

CARTER'S CHILDRENS WEAR

601 Wabash St.
Michigan City, IN 46360
219/874-4811

Save up to 60% on children's wear from this quality manufacturer. Clothing for every day of your child's life from newborn to size 14. Sleepwear and playwear in an assortment of styles and colors is available. If you're looking for the perfect baby shower gift, they also have layettes available.
Additional Location: Horizon Outlet Centers, Fremont 219/833-6425

FARAH FACTORY STORE

11626 N. E. Executive Dr.
Edinburgh, IN 46124
812/526-9500

Enjoy factory direct prices on Farah, N.P.W., and Savanne. A large selection of boys' apparel from size 4-12 and men's clothing in a variety of styles and sizes.

FLORENCE EISEMAN

601 Wabash St.
Michigan City, IN 46360
219/879-1767

Save approximately 40% from comparable retail on quality, stylish infant and children's wear. Major credit cards are accepted.

KIDS MART

7685 Shelby
Indianapolis, IN 46227
317/887-6676

Very competitively priced infant and children's clothing and accessories. They have frequent sales and often mark down this season's clothing well before the season is over. The only way to beat their sale prices is with their own discount card, which you can purchase for $6.00. You then get an additional 10% off all your purchases, including sale items, for a whole year!
Additional Locations: 5662 Crawfordsville Rd. 317/244-1400
1950 E. Greyhound Pass 317/846-7230

SMALL CHANGE

474 S. Rangeline Rd.
Carmel, IN 46032
317/843-1092

Large selection of new and used clothing from infant to size 12. You can also make substantial savings on used maternity clothing. If you need a car seat or baby bed for a short time, call and check their rental rates!

latest styles and colors. Layaway is available and they will buy, sell or trade merchandise.

MY SIZE
9911 E. 38th
Indianapolis, IN 46236
317/897-0084

The season's most stylish clothing from size 2 to 56. My Size features quality women's clothing at competitive prices.

< LINGERIE >

BARBIZON
11626 N. E. Executive Dr.
Edinburgh, IN 46124
812/526-5958

Beautiful, quality lingerie at discount prices at the big Edinburgh discount mall. A large selection of classy lingerie with savings up to 60% less than department store prices.

L'EGGS/HANES/BALI

11626 N. E. Executive Dr.
Edinburgh, IN 46124
812/526-6391

Time to update that underwear drawer! You'll be able to save up to 50% on underwear, socks, hosiery, and activewear. First quality closeouts and overstocks along with some mildly flawed merchandise.
Additional Locations: Lighthouse Place, Michigan City 219/879-5832 Horizon Outlet Centers, Fremont 219/833-3096

MAIDENFORM

11626 N. E. Executive Dr.
Edinburgh, IN 46124
812/526-9570

If it goes on first, you'll find it here. That is, if you're a woman, and it goes on first...Pay up to 60% less on bras, underwear, camisoles, half slips, and lingerie. They also offer savings on an assortment of sleepwear and day apparel.
Additional Locations: Lighthouse Place, Michigan City 219/874-3433

≺ MATERNITY ≻

DAN HOWARD'S MATERNITY FACTORY OUTLET

1280 US 31 N.
Greenwood, IN 46142
317/882-7755

Fashion at factory direct prices! A large selection of quality casual and career wear at savings up to 50% regular retail. An assortment of accessories to make the long haul a little more comfortable.

THE MATERNITY EXCHANGE

6859 Lake Plaza Dr.
Indianapolis, IN 46220
317/849-7061

The Maternity Exchange offer name brand and designer fashions at a fraction of the price you would find at specialty or department stores. They carry samples, overruns, closeouts, and irregulars in a full line of career wear, sports wear, formal wear and lingerie. You will also find the biggest selection of maternity consignment apparel in Indianapolis. In addition to all this Maternity Exchange rents formal wear for $30.00. The Maternity Exchange offers a one-stop shopping environment for the expectant mother.

SMALL CHANGE

474 S. Range Line Rd.
Carmel, IN 46032
317/843-1092

Large selection of new and used clothing from infant to size 12. Also save on used maternity clothing. If you need a car seat or baby bed for a short time, call and check their rental rates.

— *RENTALS* —

WHILE YOU WAIT

By Appointment
317/594-0599

While You Wait rents career wear and special occasion fashions for the mother-to-be. Outfits are rented on a weekly basis for a fraction of retail purchase price. They carry the latest fashions of the leading maternity wear designers in variety of sizes, a great option for women whose pregnancies span two seasons or who just need an outfit for a one-time occasion. There's no need to spend a fortune on clothing you'll only wear a few months when you can have access to such a wide variety of styles for such a relatively small amount.

≺ MEN'S APPAREL & ACCESSORIES ≻

CASUAL MALE

8275 Broadway
Merrillville, IN 46410
219/769-8290

Save up to 60% on casual apparel for men. A variety of size and current styles to choose from without having to set foot in a department store.

FARAH FACTORY STORE

11626 N. E. Executive Dr.
Edinburgh, IN 46124
812/526-9500

Enjoy factory direct prices on Farah, N.P.W., and Savanne. A large selection of boys' apparel from size 4-12 and men's clothing in a variety of styles and sizes.

GENTRY

8490 Castleton Corner Dr.
Indianapolis, IN 46250
317/849-6200

Why pay more for a label? Gentry sells clothing made by famous makers; the only difference is the Gentry label has been added. This means savings up to 40% on suits, ties, dress shirts, and activewear.

INTERSTATE JOBBERS

3335 Madison Ave.
Indianapolis, IN 46227
317/788-0566

You can double your dollar on famous-make and designer label suits from Interstate Jobbers. They offer a great selection with a sharp custom look on suits and trousers. Sizes 36 to 62 and savings up to 50%.

JOHN HENRY & FRIENDS

601 Wabash St.
Michigan City, IN 46360
219/879-6903

We found a pair of slacks whose original price was $59.50 for $39.99 here. Choose from a large selection of famous-maker men's clothing in a large assortment of sizes and styles

K & G MEN'S MART

8510 Center Run Dr.
Indianapolis, IN 46250
317/577-4245

"The best value and the largest selection of first quality men's suits, sportswear and furnishings in the state" is K & G's claim. They stock over 4,500 designer suits from $89.00 to $179.00 and over 6,000 designer ties at $7.00. They carry a large selection of discounted men's dress shirts too.

KUPPENHEIMER

4340 Lafayette Rd.
Indianapolis, IN 46254
317/299-2809

Factory direct stores. They cut out the middleman by owning their own stores and pass the savings on to you, about 40%. A crisp quality fit is easily obtained from their large selection of sizes and styles. Be sure to sign their mailing list to receive advance notification of sales and special offers.

THE MEN'S WEARHOUSE

840 U.S. 31 North
Indianapolis, IN 46142
317/881-0086

Famous-make and designer clothing and shoes at a fraction of department store prices. Alterations are available. Call 800/776-7848 for the store nearest you.
Additional Locations: 5852 E. 82nd 317/576-0558
4740 W. 38th 317/328-8095

S & K FAMOUS BRAND MEN'S WEAR

601 Wabash St.
Michigan City, IN 46360
219/879-0331

Competitive prices on famous-make men's wear. Brands include Reed, Lord and Taylor, and Hart among others. You'll also find a large selection of shirts, pants and ties.

STYLE STORE

2432 62nd
Indianapolis, IN 462
317/257-4236

Tired of finding the perfect shirt at a less-than-perfect length? Here you will find fine apparel for the big and tall man. They are family-owned-and-operated and have been in business since 1918. Visit the back room for greatly discounted men's apparel. In-house alterations available.
Additional Locations: 4909 W. 38th 317/297-1420
8540 Castleton Corner Dr. 317/842-2212

TIES, ETC.

601 Wabash St.
Michigan City, IN 46360
219/872-6661

You won't believe how many kinds of ties there are in this store! Designer silks, premium silks, price silks, poly-silks blends, extra long silks and blends, ready-tied clip-ons, tie yourself bows, banded bows, clip-on bows, and junior and boys' ties, even tie and kerchief sets. All at 40 to 70% off retail price. And, the "etc." includes belts, suspenders, hats and caps, neckwear accessories, umbrellas, and gloves. Seniors receive an additional 10% discount on Tuesdays.

VALUE CITY DEPARTMENT STORE

5100 Pike Plaza Rd.
Indianapolis, IN 46254
317/297-8808

First quality, irregulars, overstocks, and buy-out merchandise have been consolidated under one roof. They hold frequent sales in addition to their regularly low prices. Their departments include shoes, clothing, toys, sporting goods, linens, and housewares. They are also known for the famous makers suits they acquire that are sold for well below 50% of original retail.
Additional Locations: 1230 US 31 N., Greenwood 317/888-5532
6002 E. 38th 317/547-9691

WEMCO

601 Wabash St.
Michigan City, IN 46360
219/874-4434

Savings of 40 to 80% on very recognizable brand name ties and quality sportswear.

WINDSOR SHIRT
11626 N. E. Executive Dr.
Edinburgh, IN 46124
812/526-0355

Recognize the name? It's the same as the shirt from the pricey department store, but it's discounted! Windsor carries a large selection of dress and sports shirts in just about all sizes.

≺ MEN'S & WOMEN'S APPAREL ≻

BASS CLOTHING
601 Wabash St.
Michigan City, IN 46360
219/873-1783

You've known about the shoes for years; now clothing is available at discount prices. First-quality merchandise at big savings.

BOSTON TRADER
601 Wabash St.
Michigan City, IN 46360
219/873-9529

Save around 30% on Boston Trader apparel for men and women at Lighthouse Place. Major credit cards are accepted and they're open seven days a week saving you money.

BRANDS
601 Wabash St.
Michigan City, IN 46360
219/872-6396

Top brand name men's and women's apparel and accessories at 30 to 70% off retail.

BROOKS BROS.
601 Wabash St.
Michigan City, IN 46360
219/879-6777

Men's and women's career and casual wear. Quality and value for less than comparable retail.

CAPE ISLE KNITTERS
11626 N. E. Executive Dr.
Edinburgh, IN 46124
812/526-6882

The feel of 100% cotton...with savings up to 50%. Sweaters and other knit items for men and women.

EDDIE BAUER
601 Wabash St.
Michigan City, IN 46360
219/874-6178

Mostly first-quality men's and women's apparel at savings from 40 to 70%. A large selection of pants, shirts, sweaters and accessories.

FASHION MINE
825 North Crest Shopping Center
Ft. Wayne, IN 46805
317/483-3139

School clothes don't have to break the budget. Fashion Mine can save families 25% or more off manufacturer's suggested retail. There are lots of styles and colors to choose from for both misses and juniors. Watch for their sales throughout the year and save even more.
Additional Locations: 5976 US 24 W., Ft. Wayne 219/432-8611

GEOFFREY BEENE
601 Wabash St.
Michigan City, IN 46360
219/873-9527

Men's casual wear at 25 to 50% savings. American Express, Mastercard, Visa, Discover, and personal checks are accepted.
Additional Locations: Horizon Outlet Centers, Fremont 219/833-6647

HATHAWAY
601 Wabash St.
Michigan City, IN 46360
219/879-4506

Christian Dior and Speedo are among the more than a dozen labels found here. First-quality merchandise at up to 60% savings from regular retail.

J. CREW
601 Wabash St.
Michigan City, IN 46360
219/873-9292

Classic contemporary styles for men and women at savings up to 70%. A large selection of sportswear and casual wear.

JOCKEY
601 Wabash St.
Michigan City, IN 46360
219/872-5700

Save 25 to 50% on underwear, swimwear, hosiery and casual wear. First-quality men's and women's apparel. Jockey accepts major credit cards and personal checks.
Additional Locations: Horizon Outlet Centers, Fremont

JONES NY EXECUTIVE SUITS

601 Wabash St.
Michigan City, IN 46360
219/879-4789

A large selection of men's and women's suits in a variety of styles and sizes, including petites is available at Lighthouse Place. Savings average around 30%, but you'll save even more on their sale racks.

LONDON FOG

601 Wabash St.
Michigan City, IN 46360
219/872-0600

Factory owned outlet store with savings up to 50% or more on regular retail. Classic quality raingear, jackets, coats, and accessories for men and women.
Additional Locations: Horizon Outlet Centers, Fremont
3801 National Rd. E., Richmond 317/966-1021

OLGA/WARNER'S

601 Wabash St.
Michigan City, IN 46360
219/874-6706

In addition to the title brands, you'll also find Dior, Hathaway, Speedo, and White Stag labels in men's and women's apparel. Save up to 70% off regular retail.
Additional Locations: Horizon Outlet Centers, Fremont 219/833-4437

THE RIGHT PLACE

721 N. Green River Rd.
Evansville, IN 47710
812/423-5671

Save 15% or more on contemporary apparel for juniors and misses. Famous maker-brands abound, you'll be amazed how quickly the

savings add up! They're open 10:00 to 9:00 Monday through Saturday and from 12:00 to 6:00 on Sunday.
Additional Location: 2610 1st Ave., Evansville 812/474-0567

VAN HEUSEN
11626 N. E. Executive Dr.
Edinburgh, IN 46124
812/526-6220

Hordes of daughters flock here near Father's Day. They offer a large selection of men's dress and casual wear along with some accessories. Why not Mother's Day too! They carry a large array of women's activewear.
Additional Locations: Lighthouse Place, Michigan City 219/879-6744
Horizon Outlet Centers, Fremont 219/833-4029

WEARHOUSE OF FASHIONS
3680 S. East St.
Indianapolis, IN 46227
317/780-9473

Save 25% or more off department store prices on items like juniors' men's and women's clothing. They're not allowed to advertise some of the labels, but be assured you'll recognize them when you visit. In addition to accepting most major credit cards, they also have a layaway plan.

≺ RESALE ≻

— *INFANTS, CHILDREN & MATERNITY* —

ALMOST NEW SHOPPE

8974 E. 10th
Indianapolis, IN 46219
317/898-0485

Established in 1972, Almost New Shoppe sells children's and ladies' clothing and accessories. Items are offered on consignment with a 50/50 split.
Additional Location: Almost New Shoppe II, 13 Public Square Shelbyville 317/392-4114

BARE NECESSITIES

14 E. Main St.
Brownsburg, IN 46112
800/863-4333

Looking for a flower girl dress for the upcoming blessed event? Bare Necessities sells new and gently used ladies', children's, and bridal apparel. They have a diverse selection of gowns, veils, and accessories. You can also save a bundle on mothers' dresses and prom dresses here.

BEAR'S REPEATING, INC.

8150 Bash Rd.
Indianapolis, IN 46250
317/845-5354

Baby equipment, toys, children's clothing and maternity clothing are on sale here in Castleton, all at great savings below retail. Bring in your gently worn children's clothing and they'll pay cash.

CASEY'S CLOSET

5206 N. College
Indianapolis, IN 46220
317/283-3319

"The most unique children's shop in town," featuring better label and designer maternity and children's apparel. They also sell toys and accessories. Only items in exceptional condition are accepted for resale.

THE CHILDREN'S PATH

1101A North Third
Terre Haute, IN 47804
812/234-PATH

No consignments here. They pay cash for top quality children's clothing. Open six days a week, closed on Sunday.

THE CLOTHES LINE

541 E. Main St.
Brownsburg, IN 46112
317/852-5708

"A better consignment shop." They specialize in women's and children's clothing and pride themselves in the quality and condition of their merchandise.

KIDS KLOSET

6137-G Crawfordsville Rd.
Speedway, IN 46224
317/484-1821

Save everyday of the week. Kids Kloset buys and re-sells quality children's clothing, toys, furniture, equipment, and other merchandise at affordable prices. Cash is paid on the spot for used merchandise. Expect to find 50 to 75% off the original cost of an item you purchase. "Anything you might find in a kid's closet, you will find at Kids Kloset."

KIDDIE KLOTHES

621 Main St.
Beech Grove, IN 46107
317/781-8260

A quality resale store serving the Beech Grove area since 1989. Here you will find a wide selection of infant's and children's clothing and accessories for a fraction of their original cost. They're open from 10:00 to 4:00 Tuesday through Saturday.

KIDS-N-MORE

4444 N. Franklin Rd.
Lawrence, IN 46226
317/545-1309

Major credit cards are accepted here, but you may not need them with Kids-n-More's low prices. They buy and sell quality kids' and maternity apparel, toys, baby items, and accessories.

KOOL KIDS KOTTAGE

11222 Allisonville Rd.
Fishers, IN 46038
317/578-2391

"The fun place to shop" is the slogan of this Northside resale outlet. They sell quality pre-owned children's clothing sizes 0 to 14, toys, shoes, maternity and accessories. They'll pay you cash for your child's lightly worn clothes.

THE MATERNITY EXCHANGE

6859 Lake Plaza Dr.
Indianapolis, IN 46220
317/849-7061

The Maternity Exchange offers name brand and designer fashions at a fraction of the price you would find at specialty or department stores. They carry samples, overruns, closeouts, and irregulars in a full line of career wear, sports wear, formal wear and lingerie. You will also find the biggest selection of maternity consignment apparel in Indianapolis. In addition to all the sale merchandise, they rent formal wear for $30.00. The Maternity Exchange offers a one-stop shopping environment for the expectant mother.

MOTHER & CHILD RESALE SHOPPE
1746 E. 86th St.
Indianapolis, IN 46240
317/571-0115

Just found out you're pregnant? March right out and shop—but not till you drop. (You have to think of that little shopper now.) You can get off to a good start by visiting the Mother & Child Resale Shoppe. Save a ton on toys, books and clothing. They are a very friendly resale shop with everything for kids. Cash is paid for top quality items in excellent condition and they're open Monday through Saturday.

ONCE UPON A CHILD
5990 E. 71st
Indianapolis, IN 46220
317/842-0533

Once Upon a Child pays cash for just about anything pertaining to children in good condition. From clothes to toys to furniture. You can pick up several outfits for what you would pay for one at the fancy places at the crossing. New arrivals daily.
Additional Locations: 5664 Georgetown Rd 317/291-0983
South 888-7013
1204 W. 86th 317/846-7011

NANA'S
3320 Columbus Ave.
Anderson, IN 46013
317/649-8860

Nana's bills itself as "the most unique children's shop in Anderson." Nana's carries newborn to size 8 children's clothing in addition to maternity at savings from 50 to 75%. They feature a large selection of brand names, such as, Osh Kosh B'Gosh, Guess, Gap, and Bryan. They have flower girl dresses, slips, and tuxes in stock and are open from 10:30 to 5:00 Monday through Saturday. Seniors and foster parents get additional discounts.

SECOND CHILDHOOD
5140 Madison Ave.
Indianapolis, IN 46227
317/787-7333

A wide selection of infants' and children's apparel at discounted prices is available in this Southside Indianapolis store. They also sell toys and accessories. Open Monday through Friday 9:00 to 7:00 and from 9:00 to 5:00 on Saturday.

SMALL CHANGE
474 S. Range Line Rd.
Carmel, IN 46032
317/843-1092

Large selection of new and used clothing from infant to size 12. You can also save on used maternity clothing. If you need a car seat or baby bed for a short time, call and check their rental rates.

TREASURE ISLAND KIDS
9731 E. Washington
Indianapolis, IN 46229
317/895-0860

In addition to clothing, Treasure Island Kids also sells toys, furniture and accessories. Major credit cards are accepted and they're open Monday through Saturday from 10:00 to 6:00.

— *FAMILY* —

A SECOND TIME AROUND

518 E. Jefferson
Tipton, IN 46072
317/675-2380

Open Tuesday through Saturday, A Second Time Around buys and sells clothing for men, women and children, including large sizes. "Your needs are our concern" is their motto.
Additional Location: 416 Arnold Crt., Kokomo 317/455-3373

DYNAMITE KIDS RESALE

11 S. Main
Fortville, IN 46040
317/485-6011

Values are exploding here. Save up to 75% on ladies', kids', men's, maternity, and plus sizes. Dynamite Kids carries a large selection of fancy dresses and christening gowns. They're open Monday through Saturday.

GERTIES

116 E. Washington St.
Greensburg, IN 47240
812/663-3019

Top quality apparel for the family at great savings from retail. They're open Monday through Saturday and accept most major credit cards.

MEMORIES

1121 S. Range Line Rd.
Carmel, IN 46032
317/846-6286

"Tired of paying outrageous prices for clothing?" Yes! Designer label, top quality apparel for women, maternity and children. They also offer a selection of accessories.

NEXT-TO-NEW SHOP
6180 Hillside Ave.
Indianapolis, IN 46220
317/253-6746

Clothing the whole family, Next-to-New is a complete resale and consignment shop. Shopping resale shops is not only a great way to recycle; at the Next-To-New Shop, it's also a great way to help the community. Their proceeds are donated to local charities.

PUTTIN' ON THE RITZ
8816 Southeastern Ave.
Indianapolis, IN 46239
317/862-2741

This stuff isn't new? You could have fooled us. Top quality apparel in excellent condition for men, women, and children.

REPEAT BOUTIQUE
5149 US 41 S.
Terre Haute, IN 47802
812/299-9757

"A quality ladies', men's and children's resale shop." In fact, 3,000 square feet of quality resale is here, including a variety of brand names and styles for the whole family. They specialize in new maternity and wedding dresses and they're open seven days a week! Major credit cards, checks, and layaways are accepted.

SECOND SEASON
419 N. Vine
Shelbyville, IN 46176
317/398-3607

A quality resale shop featuring men's, women's and teen apparel. Formals, wedding gowns, uniforms, plus sizes, and even scoutwear. If you want it, more than likely, they have it. Aigner, Bugle Boy, Smith & Jones, Botany 500, and Naturalizer are only a few of the famous make labels you will find here. Second Season is open Tuesday through Saturday.

— MEN —

HIS FRIEND'S CLOSET

6415 Ferguson St.
Indianapolis, IN 46239
317/253-2533

Dedicated to men's consignment, His Friend's Closet has been serving Indy since 1989. Expect to save 60 to 75% on better label and designer label men's apparel. This shop is especially known for their selection of salesman's designer sample ties.

STUDLEY DUDS

2435 E. 65th
Indianapolis, IN 46220
317/255-0059

From better labels to designer labels, Studley Duds offers quality men's apparel at great savings. Consignments are done by appointment and they offer a 50/50 split!

— MEN & WOMEN —

FIRST IMPRESSION

1724 E. 86th
Indianapolis, IN 46240
317/843-2283

Specializing in quality resale for men and women, at First Impression you'll find current fashions for far less than department store prices.

RERUNS *

1039 Broad Ripple Ave.
Indianapolis, IN 46220
317/254-1444

Reruns Resale Clothiers for men and women is the only store in Indy that pays cash up front, rather than consignment, for men's and women's designer labels. Because sellers get money now, they get the best of the best—Anne Klein, DKNY, Liz Claiborne, Armani, Hart, Brooks Bros., Jones NY, Redwood & Ross, and many, many more. Named "best new resale store" in 1992 by *Indianapolis Magazine*, they have five or six "50% off" sales per year. The only way to find out about them is to be on their mailing list. After 90 days on the floor all clothes hit a 75% rack, where they usually sell for about $2.00 to $10.00.

WEAR ME OUT

920 Westfield Blvd.
Indianapolis IN 46220
317/251-4298

"A unique consignment boutique specializing in men's and women's clothing and accessories," is how this store advertises itself. Wear me out is open Monday through Saturday 10:00 to 6:00 with extended hours in the summer.

— *WOMEN & FORMAL* —

ANNIE'S APPAREL RESALE SHOP

5638 W. Washington
Indianapolis, IN 46219
317/356-6749

"Large selection of current junior style sportswear and dresses." Sounds like a good place to start slashing the school clothes' budget. They also feature famous brands in ladies fashions at great savings.

BARE NECESSITIES

14 E. Main St.
Brownsburg, IN 46112
800/863-4333

Looking for a flower girl dress for the upcoming blessed event? Bare Necessities sells new and gently used ladies, children, and bridal apparel. They have a nice selection of gowns, veils, and accessories. You can also save a bundle on mothers' dresses and prom dresses here, too.

CLASSIC COLLECTIONS

1701 Riley Rd.
New Castle, IN 47362
317/521-4435

Classic Collections is a small, Victorian-style consignment boutique, which specializes in ladies' current fashions and accessories. Elaborate displays tempt and tantalize, while their prices excite the bargain hunter. Save 40 to 75% off regular retail on quality brand name and designer ladies' apparel. "Regulars" often bring out-of-state guests in for a tour through the most unique little shop in town! Classic Collections is open Monday through Saturday from 10:00 to 5:00. Save even more with the frequent buyers' card.

THE CLASSY LASSIE CONSIGNMENT

520 N. SR 135
Greenwood, IN 46142
317/882-4310

Consignment shopping is not only economical at The Classy Lassie, with savings from 50 to 75%, but it's also fun. Each month clothing marked with a different color tag is 20%. Their quality clothing is neatly arranged and organized so you'll quickly be able to find that perfect outfit. They're open Monday through Saturday and accept layaways and major credit cards.

CLOTHES ENCOUNTERS

1454 Main St.
Speedway, IN 46224
317/244-6822

In business since 1988, Clothes Encounters saves its customers 25 to 50% on quality apparel. Save an additional 50% on certain color tags everyday! They're open Monday through Saturday. Mastercard, Visa and layaways are accepted.

CONSIGNOR CLOTHES

8055 Madison Ave.
Indianapolis, IN 46227
317/887-6787

With over 3,500 square feet of upscale resale, Consignor carries women's career and casual wear, purses, shoes and accessories. They even have maternity, wedding gowns, veils and formals. Consignor Clothes has been in business since 1986; open seven days a week. There is always a selection marked down by 50 to 75%.

DESIGNER OUTLET

1349 W. 86th
Indianapolis, IN 46260
317/255-3228

"Your closet outlet." Top quality, better-label to designer-label apparel for women. A large selection of styles and sizes offered on consignment.

LADYBUGG

5436 Columbus Ave.
Anderson, IN 46013
317/649-5288

Buying and selling ladies' apparel and accessories, Ladybugg is open Monday through Saturday. Whether it's vintage or new, they accept quality merchandise in top condition. For your convenience, they also accept credit cards.

NEW BEGINNINGS
1726 E. 86th Suite B
Indianapolis, IN 46240
317/571-0959

Don't spend a fortune on wedding apparel when you can buy a masterpiece that someone else has only worn once! In addition to wedding gowns, New Beginnings also carries a large selection of accessories. Whether it's a formal or informal wedding, you will be able to find a gown here for a fraction of the cost.

RITZY BITZY
6915 Lake Plaza Dr.
Indianapolis, IN 46220
317/842-5211

Ready to trade in your old wardrobe for a new one? You can do it with one stop at Ritzy Bitzy. They accept consignments, by appointment, on a 50/50 split. Their merchandise is top quality better labels and designer clothes and they're open Monday through Saturday.

SHERRY'S
4301 W. Clara Lane
Muncie, IN
317/289-1000

"Featuring quality ladies' apparel for today's modern lifestyles." That about sums it up, except for the fact that they pay 50 to 65% for your quality items. Sherry's is open Tuesday through Saturday from 10:00 to 7:00.

SNOOP COOP

6419 Carrollton
Indianapolis, IN 46220
317/255-0402

Some value-seekers consider Snoop Coop one of the "best kept secrets" in Indianapolis specializing in women's clothing and accessories. They offer the largest selection of sample dresses, sportswear, and lingerie, as well as top quality women's consignment. Sizes range from 4 to 18 including some petites and some large sizes. The merchandise includes one-of-a-kind, name brand fashions at discounted prices. Almost a quarter of a century in business, Snoop Coop resides in one of the oldest houses in Broad Ripple. Be sure to visit on New Year's Day for an unheard of retail sale—find what you want and make them an offer. A great day for fun and lots of bargains! The unique style of early 1900s architecture adds to the fun and mystique of "snooping" the Snoop Coop.

THE TOGGERY *

6349 N. Guilford Ave.
Indianapolis, IN 46220
317/257-5661

Quality better-label and designer clothing for 66% or more off the original prices. Six times a year you can save an additional 20 to 70%. Major credit cards, checks, and layaways are accepted and they're open seven days a week. Be sure to clip the coupon in the back for additional savings!

TOWN & COUNTRY CLOTHESLINE

9450 Haver Way
Indianapolis, IN 46240
317/575-9157

A large selection of samples, closeouts, and consignments of quality casual, career, and evening wear. They're open from 11:00 to 5:00 Tuesday through Saturday.

YOUR FRIEND'S CLOSET

6419 Ferguson St.
Indianapolis, IN 46220
317/253-3566

At this unique boutique you will find designer labels from the closets of some of the best dressed women in Indianapolis. Save 60 to 95% from the original cost of quality better label clothing. They have special sales everyday and after an item has been in the store for over a month it is discounted again. They're open Tuesday through Saturday from 10:00 to 6:00. Serving Indianapolis since 1986.

< SERVICES >

— *ALTERATIONS* —

EASTGATE TAILORS

7150 E. Washington
Indianapolis, IN 46219
317/353-1611

Pants need repair now? No problem for Eastgate Tailors. They are a full service tailor offering a range of services from reweaving to sewing buttons in place.

INTERNATIONAL ALTERATIONS

1222 W. 86th
Indianapolis, IN 46032
317/575-0275

Bring in your article in need of repair to this North Indianapolis spot, and you'll be surprised how quickly you get it back and at how low the bill is!

MAIN STREET ALTERATIONS

50 S. Madison Ave.
Greenwood, IN 46142
317/882-7120

Main Street Alterations does everything you can—without costing much more.

SUNNY ALTERATIONS

4850 S. Emerson Ave.
Indianapolis, IN 46203
317/782-0807

Did your diet plan fail you? Clothes too tight? With Sunny Alterations' very affordable rates, you can afford to let your wardrobe out to be altered. It's much less expensive than buying new clothes and you won't have to part with your old favorites.

— DRY CLEANING —

40 MINUTE CLEANERS

7017 Madison Ave.
Indianapolis, IN 46227
317/782-3859

Any guesses on how long it takes to get a garment cleaned here? The sweepstakes is on. 40 Minute Cleaners specializes in prompt service at affordable prices. If you're not in any hurry to get your order back, don't worry. They'll hold it until you get there.

KARSTADT-REED CLEANERS

1449 N. Illinois
Indianapolis, IN 46202
317/634-5333

Just around the corner from their 100th year in business, Karstadt-Reed has been saving Hoosiers money for a long time. They offer free pick up and delivery, but you can save even more (up to 20%) by dropping off and picking up the item yourself.

SCOTTEE CLEANERS
3535 S. East St.
Indianapolis, IN 46227
317/784-2642
800/953-6622

"We remove the stain your cleaner couldn't…free" is their motto. This Southside company had gained popularity throughout the whole city. If they're long distance from where you live, use their toll-free number. Scottee specializes in wedding gown preservation and stain and odor removal.

SPEED QUEEN FABRIC CARE CENTER
311 S. 1st Ave.
Beech Grove, IN 46107
317/784-2896

For slightly more than what it costs to clean one suit at full service cleaners, you can clean a couple of weeks' worth of clothing here. You do all the work yourself, from stain removal to pressing. Their staff is very helpful and they supply you with everything you need. One load is almost eight pounds of clothing and costs around $9.00. If you don't have enough for a full load consider going in with a friend, because you're charged for the full load regardless of whether you have one garment or the max.

≺ SWIMWEAR ≻

BEACH BABY SURF & SWIM SHOP
Greenwood Park Mall
Greenwood, IN 46142
317/889-1136

There's nothing more frustrating than facing the swimsuit store mirror in the spring. At Beach Baby's, they give you the option to customize with their "Create-Your-Own-2 Piece". You can match any size bottom with any size bottom and— ta-da, a bathing suit that fits!

CIRCLE CITY SWIM & SPORTSWEAR
5036 E. 62nd
Indianapolis, IN 46220
317/257-7946

Here's something you won't find in most department stores...bathing suits for sporting competition. Circle City has a full line of competitive swimwear as well as fashion bathing suits. They also carry a large selection of sportswear.

KAST-A-WAY
1728 E. 86th
Indianapolis, IN 46240
317/848-5263

Competitive swimwear at competitive prices. Don't worry if your swimming skills aren't up to competition, you'll also find fashion swim suits here. They carry a complete line of swimwear for the entire family.

KELLEHER SWIMWEAR
1908 E. 62nd St.
Indianapolis, IN 46220
317/253-4200

It's the dead of winter, you're getting ready to go to catch a few rays in Lauderdale. You need a new bathing suit, not to mention you're as white as the under underbelly of a fish. What to do? Get a new fashion swim suit at Kelleher. You'll find a great new suit, and maybe no one will notice the blinding bright glare coming out around it. They also carry a full line of accessories and mastectomy swimwear.

≺ UNIFORMS & PUBLIC SAFETY ≻

SEES EQUIPMENT & SUPPLY

8116 Zionsville Rd.
Indianapolis, IN 46258
317/875-6038

A full line of uniforms and public safety products for police, fire, EMS, and security personnel. Competitive prices on items like Berretta firearms, Code 3 products, and Bates Shoes.

THE UNIFORM HOUSE

1927 N. Capitol Ave.
Indianapolis, IN 46202
317/926-4467

This place has one of the largest inventories in the Midwest. Uniforms in all price ranges and all professions, police, nurse, fire, waitress, postal and civil defense uniforms among many, many others are available here.

ZUCKERBERG'S UNIFORMS

1518 E. Washington
Indianapolis, IN 46201
317/634-2342

If you can' t find the store, just stop and ask the nearest police officer; chances are he'll know where it is, because he shops there. Zuckerberg's has a complete inventory of uniforms and accessories for police, security, firemen, postal workers and more.

< VINTAGE & ALTERNATIVE APPAREL >

FUTURE SHOCK

6323 Ferguson
Indianapolis, IN 46220
317/251-6957

Save 5 to 30% on Airwalks, Converse, Vans, and many other brand names. This shop in the coolest part of cool Broad Ripple carries the largest collection of Dr. Martens in Indiana. Since 1988, Future Shock has been carrying a very large selection of alternative clothing and jewelry, including body jewelry. Students get a 5% discount.
Additional Location: 101 E. Kirkwood, Bloomington, 812/336-7981

RED ROSE VINTAGE CLOTHING

834 E. 64th
Indianapolis, IN 46220
317/257-5016

Since 1979, Red Rose has carried a full line of men's and women's clothing from the 1930's to the 1950's with occasional selections from 1890's through the 1920's. They are known for the good condition and quality of their merchandise. They specialize in costume jewelry with hundreds of "one-of-a-kind" pieces to choose from. Purses, hats, and shoes complete their inventory. If you need a cashmere topcoat, alligator purse, or a dressmaker wool suit with hand made button holes and silk lining—check them out! Major credit cards are accepted and they are open Monday through Saturday.

≺ WESTERN APPAREL ≻

D & J'S WESTERN WEAR

122 E. Main St.
Carmel, IN 46032
317/846-5452

The latest styles in men's and women's Western wear from boots to hats, and everything in between. They also carry an array of accessories and jewelry and can provide you with local dance and club information.

GREAT WESTERN BOOT CO.

9455 Haver Way
Indianapolis, IN 46240
317/848-1020

"Great selection! Great Prices!" Over 10,000 pairs of boots in stock including famous makers like Dingo, Tony Lama, and Stetson. They accept "Mastercard, Visa, American Express, Discover, Cash, Check, or Gold Dust."

WILD & WONDERFUL WESTERN WEAR

7150 E. Washington St.
Indianapolis, IN 46219
317/352-1564

Head 'em up and move 'em out to Wild & Wonderful Western Wear, where they have an extensive selection of men's and women's apparel and accessories.

< WOMEN'S APPAREL >

ADOLFO II

601 Wabash St.
Michigan City, IN 46360
219/872-9388

Save up to 50% on Dressy Tessy, Donna Tora and Adolfo II among others. All direct from the manufacturer to save you money and keep you on the cutting edge of style.

AILEEN STORES

11626 N. E. Executive Dr.
Edinburgh, IN 46124
812/526-2780

For those who stand by "Be American, Buy American" there's a lot to salute at Aileen Stores. From junior sizes to women's sizes, you'll save up to 70% on first-quality apparel.
Additional Locations: Lighthouse Place, Michigan City 219 872-7117
Horizon Outlet Center, Fremont 219/833-4300

ANKO ALSO

601 Wabash St.
Michigan City, IN 46360
219/874-2831

ANKO is the signature collection by Dutch designer Anneke Dekker-Olthof. Trained in Europe and established professionally in South Africa, she has been producing this exquisite collection in the U.S. since 1982. Her collection is sold in specialty shops throughout the country, but you can purchase her apparel at savings of 50% or more at two stores. In addition to the store's regular low prices, there are also sale racks where you can save an additional 20 to 50%. Look for the "back rack" where merchandise is continually marked down until it's sold. Quality workmanship is obvious on all pieces. The ANKO ALSO label

is only available at the ANKO ALSO location.
Additional Location: ANKO Fashions Inc., 731 Franklin Square, Michigan City 219/874-2288

ANNE KLEIN

601 Wabash St.
Michigan City, IN 46360
219/879-5028

From fragrances to apparel, expect to find savings up to 50% on first-quality merchandise from one of America's foremost designers.

AUREUS

601 Wabash St.
Michigan City, IN 46360
219/879-1238

Save an average of 40% on women's casual wear and separates. Head towards the clearance racks and save as much as 90%! Major credit cards and personal checks are accepted.

CAROLE LITTLE

601 Wabash St.
Michigan City, IN 46360
219/872-4341

Designer apparel for 30% less? You bet! Save on first-quality and irregular casual, career, and evening wear. If an item sticks around long enough to make it to the clearance rack you will save as much as 75%!

CHAUS

601 Wabash St.
Michigan City, IN 46360
219/874-5230

Cut about a third from your career wear budget! First-quality clothing in a variety of sizes, including petites, for women at great savings.
Additional Locations: Horizon Outlet Center, Fremont 219/833-3008

CLIFFORD & WILLS
601 Wabash St.
Michigan City, IN 46360
219/873-9522

Save 30% or more on Clifford & Wills clothing for women. Their selection includes separates, career wear, and casual wear in a variety of sizes.

DONNA KARAN
601 Wabash St.
Michigan City, IN 46360
219/874-7177

You'll save about one third with styles ranging from the cutting edge of contemporary to timeless elegance. You'll find a variety of sizes with something to fit just about everyone's taste.

FASHION SHOP
409 S. Meridian
Greenwood, IN 46142
317/882-5532

Known far and wide for their New Year's Sale, when prices are slashed by 50% off retail. Fashion Shop also has a reputation for offering everyday low prices on missy and women's apparel. Save 20 to 70% off retail on activewear and career wear. You'll find names you recognize and people you know there.
Additional Locations: 6230 Allisonville Rd. 317/251-0590
3136 N. National Rd., Columbus, 812/376-9494
2520 E. 3rd St., Bloomington, 812/334-3813

HARVE' BENARD
601 Wabash St.
Michigan City, IN 46360
219/872-3566

Save up to 40% on contemporary styles of women's designer apparel and accessories. You'll also find some men's accessories.

J. H. COLLECTIBLES
601 Wabash St.
Michigan City, IN 46360
219/872-4661

They have petites among a large selection of merchandise. Save 60% on casual and career wear on sizes 2 to 16.

JAYMAR FACTORY OUTLET
601 Wabash St.
Michigan City, IN 46360
219/879-6336

Savings from 30 to 70% on famous maker apparel and accessories factory direct. Labels include Jaymar, Sansabelt, Racquet Club and more.
Additional Location: Horizon Outlet Center, Fremont 219/833-1100

JONATHAN LOGAN
11626 N. E. Executive Dr.
Edinburgh, IN 46124
812/526-8210

Save 30 to 70% on contemporary styles of women's clothing. Action Scene, R & K Collection, Misty Harbor, Villager and many more brands are all here. They also have a great selection of petite sizes in career and casual wear.
Additional Location: Lighthouse Place, Michigan City 219/879-2422

JONES NY

601 Wabash St.
Michigan City, IN 46360
219/874-8048

Jones Wear, Dior, and New York are only a few of the name brands you will find here. A great selection of famous-make women's wear at 30 to 70%!
Additional Location:
Jones NY Woman, 601 Wabash St., Michigan City 219/878-1002

LESLIE FAY

11626 N. E. Executive Dr.
Edinburgh, IN 46124
812/526-0331

Famous-make career wear and separates for women, all at dramatic savings.
Additional Location: Horizon Outlet Center, Fremont 219/833-3020

WESTPORT WOMAN

601 Wabash St.
Michigan City, IN 46360
219/873-9580

Save up to 50% on famous label career wear, activewear, and separates for women. Their selection includes a large variety of women's sizes and accessories.

WESTPORT, LTD.

11626 N. E. Executive Dr.
Edinburgh, IN 46124
812/526-0131

Factory direct prices on career wear and activewear in current styles for women. Sizes include 4 to 14, with large selection to choose from.
Additional Locations: Lighthouse Place, Michigan City 219/872-3213
Horizon Outlet Center, Fremont 219/833-6225

COMPUTERS

< NEW & USED HARDWARE >

COMP USA

8280 Castleton Corner Dr.
Indianapolis, IN 46250
317/578-4393

Truly a computer superstore. They sell everything you need from desks to mouse pads. The prices are very competitive and they keep most everything in stock.

HARD WAREHOUSE

7779 US 31 S
Indianapolis, IN 46227
317/885-9000

A very friendly and knowledgeable sales staff welcomes you at this store. If they don't know the answer to your question, they'll find it out for you. They take a very straight forward approach to computers that customers find very helpful. At Hard Warehouse they are not shy about their prices, they invite you to take a price list with you.

SECOND BYTE USED & NEW COMPUTERS

5972 S. Madison Ave
Indianapolis, IN 46227
317/791-9999

Whether you're a computer novice or a wild-eyed hacker, check this place out. They are dedicated to customer satisfaction and are there for support long after the sale. You'll find a very knowledgeable sales staff, low, low prices on a wide variety of machines in stock and their service can't be beat. On average, you will save 20 to 50% off comparable retail! If they're not in your neighborhood now, more than likely they will be soon—this company is going places!

< SOFTWARE >

BEST BUY
562 Fry Rd.
Greenwood, IN 46142
317/881-0898

Hundreds and hundreds of titles to choose from for your IBM clone or Mac. Best Buy also has a large selection and frequent specials on complete systems. They have a large service department and offer extended warranties on most merchandise. Best Buy has locations across the state and throughout the country.
Additional Locations: 9977 E. Washington 317/897-3941
5820 E. 82nd 317/841-0711
5402 W. 38th 317/290-1330

DISKOUNT SOFTWARE
3440 N. Shadeland Ave.
Indianapolis, IN 46226
317/547-0059

Many people have computer programs and games they don't use. At Diskount Software you can bring them in and trade them for something different! They buy, sell, and trade used (and some new) IBM software. Specializing in IBM games, they carry all types of programs up to 95% below original suggested retail price. They also carry several CD Rom programs and can special order for you at discount prices. The store is a little difficult to find, but don't give up, their door faces 34th St. and they're located in the same building as an antique mall.

EGGHEAD SOFTWARE

5846 E. 82nd
Indianapolis, IN 46240
317/842-0394

With over 200 stores nationwide, Egghead can offer savings up to 50% of manufacturer's suggested retail price on brands like Ashton Tate, Hays, Lotus, and Microsoft. If you find a piece of software someplace else for less, they will not only meet the price, but beat it by $1.00. Can't beat that!

SOFTWARE ETC.

6101 N. Keystone
Indianapolis, IN 46220
317/251-3198

Competitive prices on hundreds of titles of software, video games, computer books and magazines. Can't find a particular title? Call and check with Software Etc. They also sell computer supplies and accessories and are open seven days a week.
Additional Location: Castleton Square 317/576-0260

TELECENTRAL C-D ROM SOFTWARE

6350 W. 37th
Indianapolis, IN 46224
317/328-9917

Hundreds and hundreds of titles to choose from—all for 30% to 70% below retail. Selections from categories including reference, games, business, adult titles (with proof of age), and more. Their support staff, with over 50 years combined experience, will continue to help you long after the sale. If you should find a lower price advertised someplace else, call them, they promise to beat it.
Additional Location: 10 S. Johnson Ave. 317/351-9917

WALDENSOFTWARE

3919 Lafayette Rd.
Indianapolis, IN 46254
317/299-9288

"All software and video games discounted everyday," says this branch of the major book retailer. They carry software for IBM, Macintosh, Nintendo, Sega, Amiga and others. Phone orders are accepted and if they don't have an item in stock, they will special order it for you. Become a Preferred Customer and save even more!

COMMUNICATIONS

< CAR PHONES, PAGERS & VOICE MAIL >

INDIANA PAGING NETWORK, INC.

5435 N. Emerson Way, Suite 345
Indianapolis, IN 46226
317/546-6650
800/228-2011

Locally-owned and operated since 1965, Indiana Paging Network, Inc. provides Indiana's largest continuous paging area including Louisville and Chicago. Ask about their free trial period. They offer quantity discounts and purchase specials on all of their alphanumeric, digital, tone and voice pagers. Don't fret if you need your pager serviced; they offer same day repair on all of their Motorola equipment.

MOBILECOMM

8660 Guion Rd.
Indianapolis, IN 46268
317/876-8700

Need to keep in constant touch with business associates or family members? MobileComm has local, regional, and nationwide coverage plans to meet your needs. Ask them about their discount price plans and quantity discounts.

VOICE ONE

7168 Zionsville Rd.
Indianapolis, IN 46258
317/297-6655

Voice One offers a variety of plans, one of which is sure to fit your needs. Discounts are given to members of some professional organizations—be sure to ask!

ANSWER INDIANA
7311 E. 43rd St.
Indianapolis, IN 46234
317/545-1419

Whether you're in the market to buy a pager or rent one, be sure to check the prices at Answer Indiana. They also offer competitive rates on voice mail and paging is made easy with their quarterly billing.

DEPARTMENT STORES

BURLINGTON COAT FACTORY

7150 E. Washington St.
Indianapolis, IN 46219
317/352-9166

Cut your clothing budget to a fraction of its former self. And your housewares budget. And your baby budget. And your costume jewelry budget and all of your other budgets. Here you will find the latest styles and quality goods for less!
Additional Location: 8275 Broadway, Merrillville 317/736-0636

MARSHALL'S

5120 W. 38th
Indianapolis, IN 46254
317/297-1025

Jewelry, accessories, family apparel, linens, prints, housewares: this is only a sample of the inventory at Marshall's. The inventory is constantly updated and you'll find first-quality merchandise with better and designer labels at greatly reduced prices.
Additional Location: Castleton Square 317/849-8479

SMARTS OUTLET CENTER

6900 N. Michigan Rd.
Indianapolis, IN 46268
317/259-1237

Smarts is the discount house of discount houses. Most items start at 50% below their original price. Merchandise from around 600 Target stores is filtered into this location. The best part is clothing is re-introduced in the appropriate season, so you can actually save money on winter clothes in the winter! In addition to clothing for everyone in the family, including maternity, they also have a vast assortment of household goods from decorating items to lawn care products.

STEIN MART
1488 W. 86th
Indianapolis, IN 46260
317/228-0228

First quality merchandise at very competitive prices. Departments include clothing, shoes, housewares and accessories. We recently found a toddler outfit here for $15.00 that sold at another department store for $24.00. We were especially impressed by the large selection of adorable boys clothing. Those of you who have puzzled over shopping for a boy will understand our enthusiasm! This a great place to pick up gifts for all of the showers and wedding you keep getting invited to.

VALUE CITY DEPARTMENT STORE
5100 Pike Plaza Rd.
Indianapolis, IN 46254
317/297-8808

First quality, irregulars, overstocks, and buy-out merchandise consolidated under one roof. They hold frequent sales in addition to their regularly low prices. Departments include shoes, clothing, toys, sporting goods, linens, housewares, and many others. They are also known for the famous make suits they acquire and sell for well below 50% of original retail.
Additional Locations: 1230 US 31 N., Greenwood 317/888-5532
6002 E. 38th 317/547-9691

ELECTRONICS

≺ PARTS, SUPPLIES, & EQUIPMENT ≻

ALLIED WHOLESALE ELECTRICAL SUPPLY INC.
3562 W. 10
Indianapolis, IN 46222
317/637-5151
800/875-8742

Allied caters to wholesale and retail customers and they're open six days a week. If you live outside Indianapolis, you can still check their prices by using their toll free-number.

FAMOUS BRANDS ELECTRONICS
601 Wabash St.
Michigan City, IN 46360
219/879-1192

A large selection of different kinds of electronics. Toys, small appliances, stereos, and lots of other things are available. All at savings from 30 to 70% off retail. This inventory comes from overstocks, closeouts, and special purchases.

REMINGTON
601 Wabash St.
Michigan City, IN 46360
219/872-4955

Have you been using your electric razor since the Carter administration? Well, when it finally goes out, Remington can offer you a new one for a fraction of what razors cost in even discount department stores. They not only carry electrical items, but also a wide variety of personal merchandise, including Swiss Army knives for savings ranging from 20 to 60% off retail. Major credit cards are accepted.

WHOLESALE SATELLITE SYSTEMS

7165 US Highway 40
Cumberland, IN 46229
317/894-5151

Wholesale Satellite Systems gives surveys and free estimates on residential and commercial systems at wholesale prices to the public. Financing is available and they offer senior citizen discounts.

WHOLESALE VIDEO REPAIR

6335 S. Sherman Dr.
Indianapolis, IN 46237
317/787-4450

No bench fee! Wholesale Video Repair charges by the job, with no extras added on. Be sure to bring your cash or check. They keep their prices low by not accepting charge cards.

YE OLD HI-FI SHOPPE

824 E. 64th
Indianapolis, IN 46220
317/253-5480

Since 1982, this "Hi-Fi" shoppe has been selling and servicing new and used audio and video systems. If you want to upgrade, they accept trade-ins or will sell your equipment on consignment.

FOOD & BEVERAGES

PEPPERIDGE FARM

11626 N. E. Executive Dr.
Edinburgh, IN 46124
812/526-8941

Color coded savings show what you'll save on the most popular Pepperidge Farm lines. Here you'll find Goldfish, cookies, and even Godiva chocolates. How much you save depends on the color of mark they carry, but you'll often find "buy one, get one" specials. Be sure to bring cash; they don't accept checks or credit cards.

Additional Location: Lighthouse Place, Michigan City 219/872-2205

SARA LEE OUTLET

11626 N. E. Executive Dr.
Edinburgh, IN 46124
812/526-6890

Keeping your freezer stocked with beautiful and delicious cakes is possible with the Sara Lee Outlet. Next time you're invited to someone's home for dinner, just grab one of these goodies out of the freezer and head out the door! In addition to the dessert line, you'll also find microwaveable, single-serve food and entrees that only need to be baked and put on the table. The items carried here are usually sent here for some cosmetic flaw from the manufacturing process, but on many of the items we've purchased we couldn't figure out where the flaw was.

Additional Locations: Lighthouse Place, Michigan City 219/872-2205

≺ BAKERY GOODS ≻

COLONIAL BAKING CO., INC.
2468 Winthrop Ave.
Indianapolis, IN 46205
317/923-8761

Popular breads, snack goods, and other items at a fraction of their regular price are available six days a week at Colonial Baking Co.'s thrift shop. Many items are close to their "sell by" date.
Additional Location: 7141 W. Washington 317/243-6058

DOLLY MADISON THRIFT STORE
7420 Madison Ave.
Indianapolis, IN 46227
317/788-9227

This great place to stock up on after-school snacks saves you up to 50% or more on baked goods and snack items. Many items are close to their "sell by" date.
Additional Locations: 8015 Pendleton Pike 317/898-6665
5415 W. Washington 317/240-1062

ENTENMANN'S
5016 E. 62nd
Indianapolis, IN 46220
317/259-1862

You can save everyday on Entenmann's baked goods, but on Super Saver Wednesday you'll save even more. On Super Saver Day, all regular items are $1.29 and all fat-free items are $1.49!

ROSELYN SURPLUS
2901 N. Keystone Ave.
Indianapolis, IN 46218
317/925-3605

Indianapolis' long-time sweet tooth paradise has a surplus store.
Additional Location: 3710 E. 10th 317/635-7778

WONDER BREAD HOSTESS

4586 S. Emerson Ave.
Indianapolis, IN 46203
317/784-6900

This is a great place to pick up refreshments for a kids' birthday party or any other event. Tremendous savings, averaging 30% or more, on all of their nationally known lines including snack cakes, bread, cookies, and a variety of other items.
Additional Locations: 2201 62nd 317/251-0775

< DIETETIC, BULK, HEALTH FOODS >

GEORGETOWN HEALTH FOODS INC.

3976 Georgetown Rd.
Indianapolis, IN 46254
317/293-9525

Georgetown Health Foods has been in business for over 20 years, with a Certified Clinical Nutritionist on staff to help you. They have a good selection of natural groceries, vitamins, and sports nutrition. Senior Citizens can save even more on Tuesday and quantity discounts are available to everyone, everyday.

GOOD EARTH NATURAL FOOD CO.

6350 N. Guilford
Indianapolis, IN 46268
317/253-3709

"Over 500 items in bulk, at lower-than-supermarket prices." Good Earth also carries organic produce, supplements, and refrigerated and frozen items. A quantity discount is offered. Open seven days a week and selling below retail everyday! They also carry a selection of Birkenstock sandals.

NATURE'S CUPBOARD HEALTH FOODS
2300 E. County Line Rd. S.
Indianapolis, IN 46227
317/888-0557

A very friendly and helpful sales staff assists with a good selection of natural, healthful foods. Items ranging from bulk to frozen goods at competitive prices. Prices become even lower when you spend $40.00 or more, when a quantity discount kicks in.

NATURE'S MARKET
86th & Township Line Rd.
Indianapolis, IN 46260
317/876-3131

Fresh organic produce and meats, bulk foods and refrigerated goods are among the products offered at Nature's Market. They also sell fresh herbs, body care products, books and other items. A friendly, knowledgeable sales staff can help you with any questions you have.

VINTAGE WHOLEFOODS MARKET
7391 N. Shadeland Ave.
Indianapolis, IN 46250
317/842-1032

"Largest selection of organic produce and meats." Fresh and frozen foods, bulk and packaged goods and more. They are more than happy to offer fitness and nutritional counseling and help you pull your health plan together. They also offer a selection of body care products.

≺ ETHNIC FOODS ≻

A-1 ORIENTAL SUPERMARKET

3709 N. Shadeland Ave.
Indianapolis, IN 46226
317/546-5252

Imported foods from China, Japan, Korea, Philippines, Thailand, and Latin American countries. Now you won't have to leave ingredients out of your favorite recipes just because you can't find them!

INDY ORIENTAL GROCERY

6430 E. Washington
Indianapolis, IN 46219
317/359-2137

Water chestnuts, won-ton wrappers and more. A varied selection of imported oriental goods at competitive prices.

KIM'S ORIENTAL GROCERY

8710 E. 21st
Indianapolis, IN 46219
317/897-0678

Doing retail and wholesale business, Kim's is open seven days a week. They feature imported goods from China, Korea, Japan, Thailand, Philippines, and even India.

≺ FARM MARKETS ≻

ADRIAN ORCHARDS

500 W. Epler Ave.
Indianapolis, IN 46217
317/784-0550

A third-generation, family-owned-and-operated agricultural business on the Southside of Indy, they open by July 4th each year and, depending on the crop size, stay open through January of the following year. Their primary business is apples and fresh cider, but you will also find peaches and nectarines from their farm in Mississippi. They also sell sweet corn, melons, tomatoes, squash, sweet and hot peppers and pumpkins. In addition to their homegrown produce, they also sell a line of preserves with and without sugar and sorghum, honey, maple syrup, Marion-Kay spices and extracts, popcorn and apple butter. Before the holidays they get citrus and make gift baskets that can be shipped anywhere for holiday gift giving. For three weeks in the early fall they offer school tours for Kindergarten through 12th grade for a fee. Each year at Halloween Adrian Orchards sponsors a Giant Pumpkin contest and you and your children may bring your pumpkin and join the fun. They're known nation-wide for their fresh cider. We know of several visitors who make a pilgrimage to Adrian's whenever they come to town!

TUTTLE ORCHARD

5717 N. 300 W.
Greenfield, IN 46140
317/326-2278

Like to get up close and personal with your produce? At Tuttle Orchard you can pick your own strawberries, apples and vegetables. They also sell cider, jams, honey, and gift baskets.

WATERMAN'S FARM MARKET

7010 E. Raymond
Indianapolis, IN 46239
317/356-6995

Sweet corn, tomatoes, okra, baby lima beans, hot peppers, watermelons, canteloupe, cucumbers, cabbage, and much, much more. Watermans' unit prices are below supermarket and the produce is guaranteed fresh. To save even more buy by the bushel. Hours are seasonal, so call ahead.

Additional Location: 1100 N. New S.R. 37, Greenwood 317/888-4189

≺ GROCERY STORES ≻

ATLAS SUPER MARKET

5411 N. College
Indianapolis, IN 46220
317/255-6800

"One of Indiana's most complete catering, delicatessen, and gourmet departments." They aren't kidding! A widely varied selection of meats, produce, packaged goods, and unusual brands found nowhere else—at very competitive prices. Filet Mignot at about $4.00 a pound is only one example for their great buys.

MEIJER

150 S. Marlin Dr.
Greenwood, IN 46142
317/885-3000

Meijer, originally a Michigan-based discount grocer, discounts pre-priced national grocery items by *at least* 10%. They are also very competitive on other items and a have a very large produce department. In fact, all of their departments provide a very a large selection. Not only are their prices low, you'll also save money by only buying what you need. Just about everything is available in small, as well as large amounts. We found beautiful desserts that anyone would be proud to serve at even the fanciest of dinner parties. You can stand and watch the dessert preparation, if you like.
Additional Locations: Several throughout the state.

≺ MEAT & SEAFOOD ≻

ARCHERS MEAT PACKING

259 S. Meridian
Greenwood, IN 46142
317/881-9309

At Archer's U.S.D.A. prime and choice meats—are the specialty. They also process deer meat and have lockers available. BBQ roasters are

available for rent or they will cook a BBQ pig for you. They offer a conditional guarantee on what they sell and Mastercard and Visa are accepted.
Additional Location: 8655 E. 116th St., Fishers 317/849-1790

BLUE RIBBON MEAT CO.

4767 Southeastern Ave.
Indianapolis, IN 46203
317/356-4244

When you can get 90 days same as cash, filling your freezer is a cinch. Blue Ribbon features everyday low prices and frequent specials on sides, quarters, and meat bundles. They also process deer meat for $39.95. Blue Ribbon accepts Mastercard and Visa.

COLUMBIA FISH & OYSTER CO.

2802 W. 16th
Indianapolis, IN 46222
317/638-7966

Open Monday through Saturday, Columbia has a complete selection of fresh seafood for all of your favorite recipes.

PRIME MEATS

3719 E. 38th
Indianapolis, IN 46218
317/546-0647

Everyday low prices and frequent specials on all cuts of beef and pork are featured at Prime Meats to help you reduce one of the most expensive items in your grocery bill.

SEA ISLAND SEAFOOD

2435 N. Harding St.
Indianapolis, IN 46208
317/923-5235

Sea Island has a wide selection of fresh seafood at very competitive prices.

≺ NUTS & CANDY ≻

FANNY FARMER SHOPS

601 Wabash St.
Michigan City, IN 46360
219/872-8269

Shopping at the Fanny Farmer outlet allows you to garner savings on chocolates, truffles, jelly beans, suckers and more. They have a large selection of gift boxes and sugar-free candies.
Additional Location:
Horizon Outlet Center, Edinburgh 812/526-8256

DINNER BELL WHOLESALE

2824 Shelby
Indianapolis, IN 46203
317/788-4100

With a wide variety of candy, soft drinks, paper products, sports cards and more, they specialize in fund raising. Open to the public, Monday through Saturday 7:00 to 11:00 and on Sunday from 9:00 to 9:00.

NUTS PLUS

4217 Lafayette Rd.
Indianapolis, IN 46254
317/299-4628

Nuts Plus offers a large selection of edible nuts from near and far. Far East that is. In addition to nuts, Nuts Plus sells spices and foods from India, Pakistan and the Middle East. They're closed on Mondays.

RICHARD GREEN CO. INC.
1125 Cruft
Indianapolis, IN 46203
317/783-3178

Richard Green welcomes customers for sales of any size of imported roasted nuts.

< SPIRITS >

EASLEY'S WINERY
205 N. College Ave.
Indianapolis, IN 46202
317/636-4516

Wine with personalized labels, at surprisingly affordable prices is the great gift idea from Easely's Winery. Three is the minimum purchase when ordering bottles with special labels, but the price grows progressively less expensive with the purchase of additional bottles. They're open Monday through Saturday until 6:00. Delicious Indiana wine and a very friendly staff.

INDIANA WINE GRAPE COUNCIL
101 W. Washington Suite 1320-E
Indianapolis, IN 46204
317/481-0222

Call and ask these people to send you a brochure on Indiana Wineries. It's packed full of information about the wineries, including tours, sampling, location and more.

JOHN'S SPIRITS, DECANTERS & FINE WINES
25 N. Pennsylvania
Indianapolis, IN 46204
317/637-5759

Don't forget the wine for dinner! John's Spirits, Decanters & Fine Wines has a large selection of wines at competitive prices.

KAHN'S FINE WINE & SPIRITS

5369 N. Keystone Ave.
Indianapolis, IN 46220
317/251-9463

Indisputably Indiana's #1 wine store. Since 1978, Kahn's has been serving the Indianapolis area. They have the largest collection of wines and spirits that we've seen. An Expert sales staff will help you select a wine for absolutely any occasion. On average they sell for 10 to 25% less than the competition. Receive 10% off six bottles or more or 12% off the purchase of a solid case of wine.

OLIVER WINERY

8024 N. State Rd. 37
Bloomington, IN 47401
812/876-5800

It's worth the trip, not only for their wine, but for the beautiful scenery surrounding the winery as well. Oliver Winery offers guided tours and wine sampling.

HOBBIES

BECK'S HOBBIES OF CLAREMONT
9014 Crawfordsville Rd.
Indianapolis, IN 46234
317/297-4257

Over 1,000 plastics in stock! Beck's sells cars, planes, boats, chemistry sets, robots, stamps, and coin supplies. They're open seven days a week and major credit cards are accepted.

HOBBY MASTERS
8501 Bash Suite 700
Indianapolis, IN 46250
317/576-1961

Hobby Masters sells radio controlled cars and other hobby needs at competitive prices and offers the largest indoor track for radio controlled cars in the area. They're open everyday except Wednesday.

HOBBY R/C
1102 S. Franklin Rd.
Indianapolis, IN 46239
317/359-6242

Hobby R/C discounts planes, engines, radios, and plastics to nurture the kid in us all. They have a large selection in stock and are open Monday through Saturday.

ABC COIN, STAMP, & JEWELRY
1014 E. Troy Ave.
Indianapolis, IN 46203
317/787-4066

ABC sells all of the above plus supplies at competitive prices with helpful advice to the novice.

THE COIN INDEX

857 N. Madison Ave.
Greenwood, IN 46142
317/885-8065

The Coin Index has over 18 years of experience in coins, jewelry and precious metals and offers all of the supplies you'll need for a well organized coin or stamp collection.

ENGLE'S COIN SHOP INC.

3520 Founders Rd.
Indianapolis, IN 46268
317/875-0617

Wholesale and retail for the coin collector! With over 61 years experience in coins and precious metals, Engle's Coin Shop Inc. claims to be the "top cash buyer of coins." They're open Monday through Saturday and deal with estates and appraisal, too.

COMIC CARNIVAL & S-F EMPORIUM

6265 Carollton Way
Indianapolis, IN 46220
317/253-8882

"The first in comic specialties since 1975." Dig out the old Spiderman and Batman classics from when you were a kid, especially if you were a kid between 1938 and 1965, and trade them in for cash. Comic Carnival buys, sells, and trades old comics. You'll also find a great selection of T-shirts, imported toys and models, sports cards and supplies. Over 250,000 collector comics and new comics are same day released. There are several locations around town.

Additional Locations: 3837 N. High School Rd. 317/293-9386
982 N. Mitthoeffer 317/898-5010
5002 S. Madison 317/787-3773
7311 U.S. 31 South 317/889-8899

WINE ART INDIANAPOLIS

5890 N. Keystone
Indianapolis, IN 46220
317/546-9940
800/255-5090

"Everything for the discriminating beer and wine maker," boasts this specialty store. Wine making is made easy with exclusive grape concentration. With their beer malt extracts, you can make a beer that suits your taste perfectly.

HOME FURNISHINGS

COSCO FACTORY OUTLET STORE
Columbus Center
Columbus, IN 47201
812/372-0141

Cosco is a manufacturer of juvenile products and home furnishings and here you can save up to 30% on quality products. Founded in 1935 with a retail outlet established in 1979, they have relocated to Columbus Center to accommodate their growing customer base. A second store is planned for the Hamilton Common Outlet Center in Noblesville.

≺ CHINA, CRYSTAL, & TABLEWARE ≻

CORNING/REVERE
11626 N. E. Executive Dr.
Edinburgh, IN 46124
812/526-2678

No kitchen is complete without Corningware, glass and Revere accessories, and you can get them all at outlet prices. You will also save money on Pyrex brands.
Additional Locations: Horizon Outlet Center, Fremont 219/833-1572
Lighthouse Place, Michigan City 219/879-0636

CRATE & BARREL
601 Wabash St.
Michigan City, IN 46360
219/878-0200

Crate & Barrel is an exciting retailer of home accessories at bargain prices. Purchasing their discontinued or special purchases of merchandise you could save as much as 50% off the original price.

DANSK
601 Wabash St.
Michigan City, IN 46360
219/879-8300

Save up to 60% on flatware, dinnerware, glassware, gifts and more. Timeless Dansk designs for a fraction of regular retail.

FAMOUS BRANDS HOUSEWARES
11626 N. E. Executive Dr.
Edinburgh, IN 46124
812/526-8872

Outlet prices on famous-maker kitchenware, gadgets, accessories and more.
Additional Location: Lighthouse Place, Michigan City 219/879-0438

FARBERWARE
11626 N. E. Executive Dr.
Edinburgh, IN 46124
812/526-0025

There's money to be saved! And Faberware is the place to do it. Faberware brand cookware is sold here for less than what you would pay in a department store.

THE GLASS SHOPPE
2160 E. 116 Carmel
Carmel, IN 46032
317/844-0884

Very competitive prices on crystal, china, and decorative pieces by famous makers. A price check will show their everyday prices beat department store sale prices.

INDIANA GLASS OUTLET

1300 Batavia Ave.
Muncie, IN 47302
317/282-7047

Factory direct prices on Indiana Glass and Colonial glasswares. Discounts are at least 50% and you can find several pieces for under $1.00 in this home city of historic Hoosier glass and pottery.

KITCHEN COLLECTION

11626 N. E. Executive Dr.
Edinburgh, IN 46124
812/526-9518

First quality goods, seconds, and discontinued items for the kitchen, from functional to purely fun pieces. You'll save 20% to 70% at Kitchen Collection.
Additional Locations: Horizon Outlet Center, Fremont 219/833-4150
Lighthouse Place, Michigan City 219/874-5854

ONEIDA

601 Wabash St.
Michigan City, IN 46360
219/879-6758

Silver for less! Save 20% to 70% direct from the manufacturer. Choose from their selection of flatware and tableware.
Additional Location: Horizon Outlet Center, Fremont 219/833-1907

ROYAL DOULTON

601 Wabash St.
Michigan City, IN 46360
219/872-7916

Are you taking a trip down the aisle soon? Make gift-giving easy on your guests by utilizing Royal Doulton's national gift registry. Plus you'll save them 20% to 70%. If the wedding bells have long since passed and it's baby booties in your future, check out their selection of Bunnykins and Beatrix Potter baby dish sets.

TUESDAY MORNING

1265 N. Madison
Greenwood, IN 46142
317/885-7781

You can save up to 50% or more on just about everything for the home. Their inventory includes crystal, china, holiday decorations, rugs, and even hammocks. All this and much, much more.
Additional Locations: 110 W. Main 317/844-4192
5060 E. 62nd 317/251-7367

≺ DECORATOR ITEMS ≻

BRASS FACTORY

11626 N. E. Executive Dr.
Edinburgh, IN 46124
812/526-6281

Ships ahoy! You can stop looking for that captain's bell, because it's here. The brass factory has nautical accessories and other first-quality brass goods and features savings on all sorts of decorator items for the home and office.

SASSAFRASS

601 Wabash St.
Michigan City, IN 46360
219/872-4112

A great place to shop! Save up to 50% on a variety of goods including dishes, cookware and others. Crust mixes and pizza bakeware make pizza masterpiece creation a cinch.

VILLAGE CLOCK SHOP

7150 E. Washington
Indianapolis, IN 46219
317/359-3462

Discounted grandfather, wall and mantel clocks by famous makers. They offer statewide delivery and 90 days same as cash.
Additional Locations: 5 N. Main 317/873-3462

WACCAMAW

10435 E. Washington
Indianapolis, IN 46229
317/897-0765

Department stores, eat your hearts out! Waccamaw offers customers savings up to 80% on first-quality famous-make dishes, china, and tableware. They also have a large craft, framed art, and silk flowers department. Does saving money wear you out? Stop at the refreshment stand and enjoy a lowfat yogurt in a waffle cone.

WELCOME HOME

11626 N. E. Executive Dr.
Edinburgh, IN 46124
812/526-5760

Framed art, table linens and elegant gift items are available at competitive prices.

WOODEN BENCH

11626 N. E. Executive Dr.
Edinburgh, IN 46124
812/526-8180

Go back to the basics. Beautiful gifts and furniture with a country flair all at down home prices. See ya'all there.

≺ FURNITURE ≻

— *BEDROOM* —

BEDDING LIQUIDATORS SLEEP SHOPS

1934 N. Shadeland
Indianapolis, IN 46219
317/359-5441

"America's greatest sleep chain" tries to prove its claim everyday by offering savings of 20% to 60% on famous-make bedding. Ask about their low price guarantee. Major credit cards are accepted and next-day delivery is available.
Additional Locations: Several locations throughout Indiana.

FUTON FACTORY

7621 Shelby
Indianapolis, IN 46227
317/882-7600

Don't knock 'em 'til you tried 'em. Futons, that is. They're a surprisingly comfortable, economical, and practical solution to a guest bed problem. Stylish and very affordable sleep answers are found at the Futon Factory.

HOLDER MATTRESS FACTORY

7775 US 31 S.
Indianapolis IN 46227
317/885-8448

Are the sleepless nights due to your lumpy, broken mattress or from worrying about the cost of a replacement mattress? Since 1947, Holder has been saving Hoosiers money on quality bedding. All sizes of innerspring mattresses and box springs are sold, in addition to electric adjustable beds, genuine brass beds, wooden beds, and day beds.

— *HOME* —

ANTHONY WHOLESALE FURNITURE

4243 W. 96th
Indianapolis, IN 46268
317/876-1226

Since 1980, this family-owned and operated store has been discounting furniture. Approximately 250 brands are available at savings of about 40%. Mattresses are discounted by 50%. Frequent buyers can save even more with their frequent buyer discount. Layaway is available and credit cards are accepted.

DINETTES & MORE

88 US 31 S.
Greenwood, IN 46142
317/882-5672

Choose from their more than 100 displays or special order at no extra cost. A variety of colors, fabrics and sizes are available at competitive prices. They're open seven days a week.

EMRICH'S FURNITURE

324 W. Morris
Indianapolis, IN 46225
317/634-6304

For over a century Emrich's has been selling famous-brand furniture at competitive prices. An extra discount is always given for cash, and they offer statewide delivery.
Additional Locations: 2721 E. 86th St. 317/255-2471
100 S. Post Rd. 317/898-5957
4420 Lafayette Rd. 317/297-8890

*FURNITURE BARGAINS **

4606 N. Franklin
Indianapolis, IN 46226
317/547-3558

Whether you need one piece or house full, Furniture Bargains offers a huge assortment of furniture at of 20 to 25% below comparable retail. They sell quality products and have a friendly sales staff to assist you.

JENNIFER CONVERTIBLES

30 Monument Circle
Indianapolis, IN 46204
317/236-1607

Jennifer Convertibles provides a quality new sofabed for less than what many good used sofas or beds cost. They have over 500 styles and 2,000 fabrics to choose from.
Additional Locations: 3736 Commerce Dr. 317\299-5671
3952 E. 82nd St. 317/845-0012

KITTLE'S FACTORY OUTLET

7150 E. Washington
Indianapolis, IN 46219
317/356-5400

A slightly less fancy (and pricey) little sister of the big Kittle's offers bargains on furniture for the bedroom, living room, and the rest of the house.
Additional Locations: Southport Center 317/882-2182
Speedway Supercenter 317/247-1284

MADDEN FURNITURE

1600 N. Sherman
Indianapolis, IN 46218
317/356-2431

How can you not save money when the furniture is made on the floor above where it is sold? Madden's provides factory prices on sofas, love seats, chairs, recliners, dining tables, mattresses, end tables—the list goes on at Madden's.

MARTIN FURNITURE CO.

5420 S. US 31
Indianapolis, IN 46227
317/787-8659

Shh...It's a secret. We're not allowed to mention these famous makers by name, but they are all brands that are well known and trusted. And here they cost as much as 50% less! That even includes special orders in most cases.

NORTH CAROLINA FURNITURE OUTLET

24260 SR. 37
Noblesville, IN 46060
317/773-5453

Save money on furniture directly from the furniture capital. North Carolina sells a wide selection of first quality furniture for your home for what truly is a lot less.

OAK DESIGNS

1945 E. Stop 13 Rd.
Indianapolis, IN 46227
317/889-0380

This locally owned family business can save Hoosiers dollars on solid oak tables, chairs, china hutches, curios, desks, bedroom sets and more. Layaways are accepted for up to 9 months and there's no extra charge for special orders.

OAK EXPRESS

8310 E. Washington
Indianapolis, IN 46227
317/897-5887

Solid Oak furniture for less. Choose from their large selection of dinettes and curios. Major credit cards are accepted.

OAK OUTLET

10019 E. Washington
Indianapolis, IN 46229
317/898-4986

"Quality Oak Furniture at Outlet Prices." Oak furniture for every room of the house, except the bedroom. Layaways are accepted for 30 days with 20% down or 90 days same as cash is offered.

— REPAIR —

ACTION FURNITURE REPAIR

1118 S. Sherman Dr.
Indianapolis, IN 46203
317/357-2095

Your orange corduroy recliner is on its last leg? Don't throw it out! Action Furniture Repair advertises that it can repair furniture for far less than it would cost for a replacement. They've been in business over 37 years and specialize in refinishing, repairing, and upholstery. They even make house calls on small repairs.

— *RATTAN & WICKER* —

SCHOOL HOUSE OF EDUCATED WICKER

SR 28
Hobbs, IN 46047
317/675-2938

"A pleasant drive from anywhere." Competitive prices on classic wicker furniture for the bedroom, bathroom and other places in the home. They also sell baskets and accessories. Items are imported from all over the world. Open seven days a week.

— *UNFINISHED* —

U. S. UNFINISHED FURNITURE FACTORY *

4905 W. 38th
Indianapolis, IN 46254
317/293-5623

U. S. Unfinished Furniture Factory began selling furniture as a family business in Indianapolis in the 1970s. Two of the original family members remain active in daily operations, as the company continues to grow. Stores are well stocked and nicely decorated to show off the high quality solid wood furnishings. Both stores stock a wide selection of factory finished oak furniture as well as a complete finishing section for the do-it-yourself enthusiast. Woods of choice are oak, poplar, maple and pine with many selections in each and custom finishing is available. Many customers bring a piece of favorite furniture from home so a custom blended stain can be made to match exactly. Delivery is available for a modest charge and is always scheduled at the customer's convenience. Savings average about 20%, plus they have in-store sales and seasonal discounts.

< INTERIOR DECORATING SERVICE >

REARRANGEMENT BY DESIGN

872 Nero Crt.
Carmel, IN 46032
317/844-9221

A penny saved...Those savings really add up when you eliminate the need to purchase new items! Rearrangement By Design will save you money by optimizing the use of what you already have. This service is available to residential and commercial customers. What will they think of next!

SAVVY DECOR

1504 E. 86th
Indianapolis, IN 46240
317/848-4942

What a deal! Save 20 to 50% off retail on furniture, wallpaper and more—plus receive free decorating service! Visit their store Monday through Friday between the hours of 9:00 and 6:00. Also, Saturday from 10:00 to 6:00.

USE WHAT YOU HAVE

9158 Castlegate Dr.
Indianapolis, IN 46256
317/578-1993

Why buy new when you can use what you have? Use What You Have can help you maximize your space and create stylish design by using your existing furniture and decorating items. Prices depend on how much space is involved and the amount of moving involved. If you don't have enough to work with, they have a shopping service available to help you find what you need.

< LIGHT FIXTURES & CEILING FANS >

BEVELED GLASS & LIGHTING DESIGNS

3185 N. Shadeland
Indianapolis, IN 46226
317/547-5256

"Wholesale lighting at wholesale prices." 5,000 square feet of showroom space allows for many samples. They offer free consultation on layout.

CARMEL ELECTRIC SUPPLY

1730 E. 156th
Carmel, IN 46032
317/896-3899

Over 500 lights on display! Can't decide? Let their Certified Lighting Consultants help you choose from the selection of fixtures, lamps, recessed lighting and paddle fans. Open seven days a week.
Additional Locations: 5575 Elmwood Ave. 317/788-5832

DAN'S FAN CITY

8407 Castleton Corner Dr.
Indianapolis, IN 46250
317/842-2320

With over 200,000 possible combinations, if you don't find the fan you want here, it must not exist. Contemporary and classic designs sold at competitive prices.

EXCITING LITING LAMP & SHADE CENTERS

1774 E. 86th
Indianapolis, IN 46240
317/846-9516

With over two decades of serving Indianapolis' lighting needs, Exciting Liting offers a large selection of lampshades, floor and table lamps at competitive prices.

≺ LINENS & TOWELS ≻

FIELDCREST CANNON

11626 N. E. Executive Dr.
Edinburgh, IN 46124
812/526-2887

A king-size comforter for $19.99? We found one (and bought it) at Fieldcrest Cannon. Granted, they're not all priced that low, but they do have a great selection of all sizes for about half off regular retail. They also sell towels and accessories at great savings.

≺ RESALE FURNISHINGS ≻

BETTER HOMES & BARGAINS

2505 E. 65th
Indianapolis, IN 46220
317/255-0310

Fine Furniture for less. A large selection of furniture, housewares, and decorating items offered on consignment. Pay far less than what you would new.

CARMEL FINE FURNITURE

5 S. Range Line Rd.
Carmel, IN 46032
317/844-9594

You would never guess that these furnishings are used…everything is top-quality and in excellent condition. We should also mention that you'll only pay a fraction of the piece's original cost. Carmel Fine Furniture discounts new furniture by 25%.

HOME AGAIN - HOME AGAIN

853 E. 65th St.
Indianapolis, IN 46220
317/255-1277

This is a new concept in consignment shopping, home decor and accessories—an appealing store that looks like a fine retail shop. Everything from kitchen items to fine china is clean and well displayed. Ever-changing merchandise is a real motivation to return at least once a week, as merchandise arrives daily. Their motto is "buy that one of a kind item today...tomorrow it may be gone." Items are priced from $.50 to $2,000.00. Consignments are done by appointment only. They also offer free in-home services.

HOME FURNISHINGS WITH A PAST

5 S. Range Line Rd.
Carmel, IN 46032
317/844-9594

Home Furnishings With a Past sells a variety of quality furniture and accessories for far less than the original price. The store is jam-packed with goods in excellent condition. You wouldn't believe the turn over here, so you may need to visit often!

≺ WALL & WINDOW TREATMENTS ≻

ABC CUSTOM DRAPERIES

4202 E. New York
Indianapolis, IN 46201
317/356-6395

Here's music to our ears..."Wholesale to the public." Save money on shades, blinds, fabrics, bed linens, upholstery and even hardware.

DISCOUNT FABRICS & DISCOUNT DRAPERIES

25 E. Court
Franklin, IN 46131
317/736-6515

This store is incredible! It's one city block wide with two selling floors, for a total of 24,000 square feet of retail space. Discount Fabrics offers the widest selection of fabrics in the state and everything is discounted everyday. Every imaginable sewing need is met here—upholstery, drapery, bridal and after-five, quilt, wool, dress goods, laces, trims, and more. They have a wide selection of ready-made draperies, tiers, toppers, laces, custom cancellation draperies, and bedspreads. What if they don't have it in stock? They also discount special orders. They know they're doing their job when they see their everyday low prices are often lower than another store's advertised sale prices.

THE DRAPERY OUTLET STORE

5330 N. Tacoma
Indianapolis, IN 46220
317/254-2362

Bring in your measurements—you'll want to order when you see their large selection and low prices. If you can't come to them, they'll come to you with their shop-at-home service.

EVERYDAY PAINT & WALLPAPER INC.

1367 W. 16th
Indianapolis, IN 46202
317/635-5255

We're willing to bet that you find what you're looking for before you've finished browsing in over 2,000 wallpaper print books. They also have complete lines of paint at competitive prices.
Additional Locations: 1403 E. 86th St. 317/253-4180
1028 E. Main St, Brownsburg 317/852-0146

JOEY'S DISCOUNT WALLPAPER STORE INC.

2625 Lafayette Rd.
Indianapolis, IN 46222
317/923-4433

Over 200,000 rolls in stock! Choose from a large assortments of colors and styles at discounted prices.

MILL END

4720 N. Keystone
Indianapolis, IN 46205
317/257-4800

Your mother probably bought the family drapes at Mill End. For over a half a century Mill End has served Indianapolis. Choose from thousands of first quality fabrics at savings to 50% or more. They have their own workroom right in the building to save you money. A free shop-at-home service is available

NOT JUST BLINDS

7710 Johnson Rd.
Indianapolis, IN 46250
317/842-1044
800/2607878

Just as the name states—Not Just Blinds. They offer all your decorating needs in one place at great savings. More than 1,200 catalogues are on the shelves. They also have factory-direct prices on blinds and paints. Their on-staff decorating consultants will help you at no extra cost.

OLD BOB'S

9400 Rockville Rd.
Indianapolis, IN 46234
317/271-2266

With over 1,500 patterns of wallpaper in stock, you're bound to find what you're looking for and pay less than comparable retail. Old Bob's has competitive prices on barns, bird feeders and picture frames. They also have a large selection of paint at affordable prices.

WALLS & ALL
1960 E. Stop 13
Indianapolis, IN 46227
317/888-1111

Walls & All offers savings on wallcoverings and window treatments every day of the week! Choose from 1,000 that are in stock, or special order what you want and still get great savings.

JEWELRY

BUCKLE PLUS - DANIEL'S

11626 N. E. Executive Dr.
Edinburgh, IN 46124
812/526-0927

Buckle Plus - Daniel's offers discounted gold, diamond, and watches 10 % to 60% off retail. If you would like to recycle your existing jewelry, they also do custom designing. In addition to their name brand watches like Pulsar, Citizen, and Bulova, they have a wide selection of class and mother rings along with a full line of leather products. They carry over 3,000 buckles and will custom-size a belt while you wait.

GOLD COBBLER

1251 US 31 N.
Greenwood, IN 46142
317/881-3005

We needed a ring to be resized and they accomplished that task right on the spot for only $15.00. Gold Cobbler has sincerely terrific prices.

GOLD 'N SECRETS

301 E. Carmel Dr.
Carmel, IN 46032
317/844-7700
800/473-0710

Do people have their jewelry duplicated? Indeed they do at Gold 'N Secrets. They specialize in repairing jewelry and creating travel jewelry for the most discriminating buyer.

MCGEE & CO. FINE JEWELERS
880 US 31
Greenfield, IN 46140
317/882-0500

A large selection of watches, bridal sets, and loose diamonds with serious price reductions. In addition to their prices, McGee offers frequent specials.

ROBERT'S JEWELERS
7110 Madison Ave.
Indianapolis, IN 46227
317/788-1405

For over 53 years, Robert's Jewelers have been creating custom designs of fine jewelry. They have one-day service and it's done on the premises.

SHANE CO. OUTLET
7150 E. Washington
Indianapolis, IN 46219
317/357-0209

Fine jewelry at outlet prices.

ZEBON'E JEWELRY
3847 Moller Rd.
Indianapolis, IN 46254
317/299-7580

Zebon'e offers custom design, appraisals and wholesale prices. Need your jewelry repaired? They repair on premises and average a two-day return on most repairs.

MEDICAL NEEDS

< DRUG STORES & PHARMACIES >

F & M DISTRIBUTORS

7150 E. Washington
Indianapolis, IN 46219
317/353-1003

Save up to 10 to 70% or more on first-quality merchandise and special purchases, like health and beauty goods, household needs, edibles, paper goods and more.
Additional Locations: 8030 US 31 S. 317/887-9655
1300 E. 86th 317/571-0059

LOW COST RX

8275 Madison Ave.
Indianapolis, IN 46227
317/881-8262

How do you cut corners on your prescription bill? Low Cost RX offers prescription help for the sick budget. Save on most all your presciptions and up to 50% on generic replacements. A friendly, neighborhood pharmacy that does their best to bring you prompt, personal service at competitive prices, Low Cost RX is found in several convenient spots.
Additional Locations: 3940 S. Keystone 317/787-7205
988 E. Main St., Greenwood 317/888-5373

PHAR-MOR

8800 US 31 S.
Indianapolis, IN 46227
317/889-1159

Ask about their low price guarantee. Here you can save on everything from presciptions to health and beauty needs and they also have video rental for 98¢ for two nights! Or, you can rent three videos for about

$2.50 for two nights. That's hard to beat for a couple of nights of entertainment. Invite friends over and make it an even better value.
Additional Locations: 10235 E. Washington 317/897-1159
Lafayette Place 317/293-6175
Castleton Plaza 317/841-0393

WESTSIDE LOW COST PHARMACY
8336 W. 10th
Indianapolis, IN 46214
317/271-0071

Who says you can't get personalized service in this day and age? Westside Low Cost Pharmacy specializes in friendly, courteous service with old-fashioned prices. There's no need to wait in line all day; personalized service assures quick in-and-out. Many insurance cards are accepted for your convenience.

< OPTICAL SERVICES >

EYE WORLD
7657 Shelby
Indianapolis, IN 46227
317/881-1400

Eye World features a large selection of quality glasses for $37.88. Their contact lenses start at $69.88 and bifocals start at $79.88. They do eye exams at all locations and prices range from $33.00 to $38.00. Are things becoming clearer, yet?
Additional Locations: 5840 S. Crawfordsville Rd. 317/484-1400
7814 E. 96th 317/595-9600
3463 W. 86th 317/471-1400

SIGHT & SAVE

5146 Pike Plaza
Indianapolis, IN 46254
317/291-3848

Glasses for under $40? From the contemporary to the classic, Sight & Save has over 750 frames from which to choose. Contact lenses start at $29.96 with the exam costing $67.00 (which includes the fitting and follow-up). Bifocals start at $69.96 and the exam is only $36.00.
Additional Locations: 882 US 31 N., Greenwood 317/889-5770
9996 E. Washington St. 317/895-1250
5447 E. 82nd 317/845-9460
1422 W. 86th 317/872-4070

WEHR OPTICAL CO.

2033 E. 46th
Indianapolis, IN 46205
317/253-6887

There are still some family-owned businesses in the world! Since 1969, Wehr has been serving Indianapolis. Choose from contacts for daily wear, extended wear, disposable, cosmetic, and astigmatisms. They have contacts to fit every need. Not ready for contacts? You can save on glasses too.

≺ SUPPLIES & EQUIPMENT ≻

HOOK'S HOME HEALTH CENTER

7049 E. 10th
Indianapolis, IN 46219
317/352-1100

Taking care of a sick family member at home can be difficult. Hook's Home Health Center sells and rents products that can make life easier. Wheel Chairs, for example, rent for $25.00 a week with a refundable $50.00 deposit. They also have a variety of other products like monitors, bedding and more. Their rates are very low and the items are all in good, dependable condition.

Additional Locations: 9501 N. Meridian 317/844-8170
5229 W. Washington 317/241-5020
4200 US 31 S. 317/784-0226

MEMBERSHIP STORES

UNITED CONSUMERS CLUB

7261 N. Keystone
Indianapolis, IN 46240
317/257-7436

Have you ever wondered how buyers for retail stores choose their merchandise? The answer is through manufacturers' catalogues. You can get your hands on those catalogues at United Consumers Club, a catalogue showroom that is available to club members. You can expect to find savings from 20% to 60%. In addition, they offer even greater savings in their quarterly sale publication. They sell everything from home furnishings and electronics to recreational equipment and fine jewelry. In the back of each catalogue is the suggested retail price and the club price with either a specified percentage off retail or the listed cost of the item. Each manufacturer is able to offer these great savings to United Consumers Club because of the volume the club purchases from them. There are clubs nationwide.

SAM'S CLUB

8301 E. Washington
Indianapolis, IN 46219
317/897-2582

Sam Walton had one of the world's greatest ideas when he started this business. Sam's Club offers bulk items at great savings: everything from car tires to potato chips and clothes too. Sam's maintains their regular stock of goods and add seasonal and special buys periodically. You never know what you'll find in these sprawling mega mercantiles, and that's what makes it fun as well as economical.

MUSIC &VIDEOS

< NEW & USED >

DISCOUNT ENTERTAINMENT

601 Wabash St.
Michigan City, IN 46360
219/873-1090

Save up to 20% or more on CD's, cassettes and even videos! Discount Entertainment carries a vast collection of contemporary favorites and old classics. They accept major credit cards and are open seven days a the week.

THE FLIPSIDE

7936 Pendleton Pike
Indianapolis, IN 46226
317/542-9207

If you have a jukebox and would like to stock it full of oldies, Flipside is just the place. They carry both 45's and CD's, hard-to-find titles and jukebox title strips to make your selections look authentic. If you're out of the city, place your order over the phone and they'll ship it to you.

HALF PRICE BOOKS RECORDS & MAGAZINES

844 N. US 31
Greenwood, IN 46142
317/889-1076

See books.

MISSING LINK RECORDS

4022 Shelby
Indianapolis, IN 46227
317/782-1962

Are you an LP connoisseur and can't find new releases on vinyl? Missing link carries new and used LP's, CD's, tapes and posters and they are stocked with collectibles from the 50s to the present. We found a Talking Heads collection on CD for about half of what a local 'discount' store charges. Bravo! We've been waiting for "Valley Girl" for years and Missing Link had the CD in stock as soon as it was released.

MUSIC TO GO

4850 S. Emerson Ave.
Indianapolis, IN 46227
317/783-3287

Need money, are you tired of the same old songs? Music To Go will buy, sell, and trade cassette tapes and CD's.

POLAR BEAR RECORDS

6918 Madison Ave.
Indianapolis, IN 46227
317/783-3492

Take a little cool cash and pick out some new or used CD's, LP's, 45's and imports, for the exotic side of life. They also buy your used tunes.

TRACKS RECORDS

7683 Shelby
Indianapolis, IN 46227
317/889-0877

At Tracks Records Monday through Friday you can enjoy extra savings from 11:00 to 1:00. They always have the top Billboard hits on

sale and they have new releases and reissues every Tuesday.
Additional Locations: 5485 E 82nd St. 317/576-0404
3748 Commercial 317/293-6886

WORLD RECORD SHOPPE

4150 Lafayette Rd. Suite D
Indianapolis, IN 46254
317/293-1690

World Record Shoppe carries new and used CD's, cassettes, LP's, 45's, music posters, and T-shirts 10 to 20% off. They boast consistently low prices and the largest selection. Quality service has been their priority in the city for 15 years. Considered one of the nation's better independent music retailers, they do it all and can order any music-related items.

MUSICAL INSTRUMENTS

ARTHUR'S MUSIC STORE
931 Shelby St.
Indianapolis, IN 46203
317/638-3524

Serving Indiana for over 41 years, they definitely know the business. Arthur's carries every thing for the rock band or the high school band. They have a large display of new and used instruments. If you're interested in learning how to play an instrument, they also give music lessons.

GUITARS & MORE
2220 E. County Line Rd. S.
Indianapolis, IN 46227
317/885-8867

Having trouble picking your guitar? Choose from Guitars & More's wide selection. If it's picking, and not choosing, that's the problem, sign up for their lessons. Why not consider purchasing a guitar and save up to 10% to 35%. Frequent buyer receive extra discounts.

MUSICIANS' REPAIR SERVICE, INC.
332 N. Capitol Ave.
Indianapolis, IN 46204
317/635-6274

Needing to find a musical instrument for junior? Musicians' Repair Service, Inc. has been family-owned-and operated for 46 years offering quality musical instruments. You can expect to save over 20%, all instruments are sold on approval of the Band Director, and they offer their own in-house guarantee in addition to the manufacturer's guarantee. They also discount to frequent buyers and professionals in the trade.

PAIGE'S MUSIC

5252 E. 65th St.
Indianapolis, IN 46220
317/842-2102

For over 123 years, since 1871, Paige's Music has been keeping everyone in tune. They specialize in band and orchestra instruments. If you can't afford to buy an instrument, they offer attractive rental plans. And, if you need new pads for your flute, or other repairs made, they have a service department.

OFFICE & BUSINESS NEEDS

≺ BUSINESS MACHINES ≻

COPIER CONNECTION INC.

3401 E. Vermont
Indianapolis, IN 46201
317/328-1536

With over 20 years experience, Copier Connection offers quality reconditioned equipment at affordable prices. They have all the popular brands for less and offer rental and leasing plans. Repairs are done by factory-trained technicians at rates that are very competitive. Need a new Minolta copier for your small business? Copier Connection is an authorized small business dealer. Fax service is available.

SPRAGUE OFFICE EQUIPMENT SERVICE

825 N. Pennsylvania
Indianapolis, IN 46204
317/237-9814

"Kaput" copiers make for headaches. Sprague offers warranties and service contracts with what they sell. In addition to doing repairs, they also rent and sell new and used copiers and supplies. Sprague has over 20 years experience and they make free deliveries.

< NEW & USED FURNITURE & EQUIPMENT >

AARON RENTS & SALES FURNITURE

4407 N. Lafayette Rd.
Indianapolis, IN 46254
317/291-3422

Buy, rent, or if you can't make up your mind, rent-to-own. Aaron has factory direct prices on TV's, VCR's, beds, sofas and more. Their rates are very competitive and special package prices are offered.

CORT FURNITURE RENTAL CLEARANCE CENTER

4904 Century Plaza Rd.
Indianapolis, IN 46254
317/291-1754

Where do all of those well coordinated furniture sets you see in corporate offices come from? Well, chances are that they're rented and will eventually end up back at Cort. Once or twice a year, they have huge tent sales (one is usually held in August), and you can choose from their framed art, sofas, chairs, tables and much more—all at a fraction of original cost.

INDIANAPOLIS STORE FIXTURE CO.

418 S. Missouri
Indianapolis, IN 46225
317/634-2344

Why spend thousands and thousands of dollars on new fixtures when you can get quality used ones for so much less? Logical question. Indianapolis Store Fixture Co. will help you make your selection of fixtures for your entire business.

OFFICE FURNITURE MART OF INDIANAPOLIS

220 St. Clair
Indianapolis, IN 46204
317/636-6696

Over 35,000 square feet of new and used office furniture are on display at this big furniture warehouse. Locally owned and operated since 1964, Office Furniture Mart emphasizes personal service. In fact, if you stop in you're more than likely to see the owner himself! Save 5 to 60% off comparable retail. Cash buyers receive a 5% discount. A free minimum two-year warranty is furnished on all new merchandise and 90 days on used. Free assembly, delivery and installation are available and major credit cards are accepted. Seventy-five percent of their business is repeat business! While you're in there, take a gander at their really neat logo.

< ONE-STOP SUPPLIERS >

OFFICE DEPOT

3708 Commercial Dr.
Indianapolis, IN 46222
317/290-0430
800/685-8800

A visit to this place will show you why you'll save money on thousands of products including office supplies, furniture, business machines and printing needs. They even offer a low price guarantee. They're open seven days a week and accept major credit cards.

Additional Locations: 4032 E. 82nd St. 317/0578-8316
4200 S. East St. 317/782-3178
10255 E. Washington St. 317/895-0039

OFFICEMAX
2110 E. County Line Rd.
Indianapolis, IN 46227
317/881-6217
800/688-6278

Officemax boasts over 6,000 office products including computers, furniture, and paper products, and free delivery with a purchase of $50 or more within their delivery area. Open seven days a week, they offer low price guarantee and have a print shop with a variety of services including bending and laminating.
Additional Locations: 5617 W. 38th 317/388-1018
3810 E. 82nd 317/578-8001

< SERVICES >

— *PRINTING* —

KINKO'S COPIES
150 E. Market St.
Indianapolis, IN 46204
317/631-6862

What do you do when you're in the middle of a mound of paper work and can't leave to make copies for that big presentation tomorrow? You've seen your answer on TV. Call Kinko's. They will pick up and deliver. The more you copy, the more you save with their volume discount. They can handle oversize copies, poster, banners, and color copies. Major credit cards are accepted. Did we mention they're a college student's best friend? Why? They're open 24 hours, and they rent Macintosh and IBM.
Additional Locations: 5973 E. 82nd St. 317/849-9683
7822 E. 96th St. 317/578-3232
5030 Pike Plaza Rd. 317/297-2679

NU-WAY PRESS

3415 Madison Ave.
Indianapolis, IN 46227
317/787-0773

According to the personable folks at Nu-Way, Old Fashioned service lives! For 30 years Nu-Way has provided Indianapolis with quality and dependable service. They print letterhead, envelopes, and business cards. You can even get your wedding invitations there! They're open 9-5 Monday through Friday.

PAR PRINTED FORMS INC.

3330 Madison Ave.
Indianapolis, IN 46227
317/787-3330

Not just printed forms, but newsletters, brochures, labels, price lists, catalogues, envelopes, booklets, resumes, business cards and more comes hot off the presses at Par. They can handle jobs of all sizes and are priced competitively. Open six days a week.

QUANTITY COPY & PRINT

607 Massachusetts Ave.
Indianapolis, IN 46204
317/262-0606

A downtown location with plenty of parking? You bet! Plus, you don't have to pay a premium for your printing needs. "You're 5¢ Copy Store." Free pick up and delivery available.

— *SECRETARIAL* —

BEST WAY SERVICES
2511 E. 46th St. Suite Q 1
Indianapolis, IN 46205
317/545-BEST

If you're ready to move out of your home office and into a real office, but can't afford the cost, check out the services at Best Way Services. They offer office rental with secretaries, fax, transcription, notary, full secretarial personalized answering system, high-speed copies, resumes, and reports, also mass mailing at reasonable prices.

— *SMALL BUSINESS* —

GENERAL BUSINESS COUNSELING
2511 E. 46th St. Suite Q 1
Indianapolis, IN 46205
317/545-2379

This isn't exactly discount but believe us it can save you money—a place to call to help you get a handle on things. General Business Counseling is a nation-wide franchise committed to assisting small businesses. Learn bookkeeping made simple, tax planning, creating financial records, profit analysis and management, basically everything you keep wanting to research and implement, but just don't have the time to study on your own. General Business can teach you how to become more productive through organizational skills and sound planning.

PARTIES & CELEBRATIONS

CASH & CARRY PAPER CO., INC.

602 E. Washington
Indianapolis, IN 46204
317/632-2651

"The Original Cash & Carry," is the way this company advertises discount prices on party items, paper goods, goody bag toys, and on your wedding and party needs.

FACTORY CARD OUTLET

5926 Crawfordsville Rd.
Indianapolis, IN 46224
317/388-9277

Their "hallmark" is a huge selection of quality greeting cards at what is truly an unbelievably low everyday price of 39¢. They also have great selections in gift wrap, party supplies, giftware, and seasonal goods. Savings average 20 to 90%. Balloon bouquets and custom-made centerpieces add to the party atmosphere. A large selection of helium filled balloons are under 60¢ and Mylar balloons are only $1.69. Seniors receive 10% of their purchases all day on Wednesday.
Additional Locations: Several throughout Indiana

THE PAPER FACTORY

5736 Crawfordsville Rd.
Speedway, IN 46224
317/241-7554

The Paper Factory has a complete line of party goods for everything from weddings to luaus. They sell two-sheet, flat wrapping paper for $2.00! They also wind down large rolls of gift wrap into smaller rolls to pass savings on to their customers. There are no cardboard cores—it's all gift wrap. They specialize in balloon arrangements and centerpieces for special occasions. Savings are from 10 to 50%. Seniors get 10% on purchases of $5.00 or more on Wednesday. A Frequent Party Club

Card and Rewind Club Card can also save repeat buyers money. Case discounts are available and volume discounts are given to those with tax exempt ID numbers.
Additional Locations:
Horizon Outlet Center, Edinburgh 812/526-5096
5534 Grape Rd., Nighthawk 219/277-2763
Horizon Outlet Center, Fremont 219/833-6424
Lighthouse Place, Michigan City 219/874-8447

PARTY +

8020 US 31 S.
Indianapolis, IN 46227
317/889-2620

Save money on cups, napkins, decorations, table coverings, plastic cutlery, aisle runners, custom printing and more. Party + is ready to help you plan a 50s theme party or any other celebration with their quality inexpensive rentals.
Additional Locations: 8375 Castleton Corner Dr. 317/579-7480
9979 E. Washington 317/899-6700
5621 W. 85th 317/872-7724

≺ COSTUMES ≻

COSTUMES BY MARGIE

3818 N. Illinois
Indianapolis, IN 46208
317/925-6406

You've driven by this spot—it's the place with eight-foot bunnies or Abraham Lincoln in the window. This unique store has sales and rentals for individuals or companies. They even make mascots by special order, but, if you're looking for something easy, Margie invites you to come and see her selection of masks, beards, make-up and more.

COSTUMES UNLIMITED

4611 N. Post Rd.
Indianapolis, IN 46226
317/898-5519

Feeling unloved? Send in the clowns, and be one yourself. Costumes Unlimited specializes in affordable transformations and in clown supplies. Extended hours for Halloween costume rental.

INDIANAPOLIS COSTUME CO. INC.

619 Virginia Ave.
Indianapolis, IN 46203
317/634-2229

Indy Costume is getting close to a century of service in dressing up Indy with costumes for Christmas, Easter, Halloween, or just because you wish transformation. They even have period costumes! Need a date for the occasion? They also have ventriloquism dolls. If magic is more your speed, stop in and see the large selection of magic supplies.

LANDES COSTUME CO., INC.

811 N. Capitol St.
Indianapolis, IN 46204
317/635-3655

For eighty-odd years Landes has provided Indianapolis with instant rented costuming. Whether you're looking for Santa Claus at Christmas time or a dark creature of the night for Halloween, Landes is willing to assist.

PARTY TIME RENTAL INC.

770 N. Range Line Rd.
Carmel, IN 46032
317/844-5178

Other people's rental suit germs may give you the heebie-jeebies. Party Time guarantees clean, sanitized new or like-new costumes. Choose from their large selection for all occasions.

PET NEEDS

ANIMAL ARTS ACADEMY

14000 Promise Rd.
Noblesville, IN 46060
317/773-6550

Let's use your average, 35-pound, short-haired Fido for an example. Boarding is only $8.00 a day, with an indoor and outdoor run. If you don't need boarding, but are interested in grooming they have very reasonable rates for that too, $15.00 was a recent quote for Fido.

FISH WAREHOUSE

124 W. Carmel Dr.
Carmel, IN 46032
317/843-9584

Have you harbored a secret desire to start an aquarium but don't know where or how to get started? Fish Warehouse is the "Marine Fish Specialists." They will be able to give you expert advise and every thing to get you bubbling. They carry aquariums from 30 - 400 gallons, fresh water fish and live plants.

FOR PET'S SAKE SCHOOL OF GROOMING

111 W. Main St.
Carmel, IN 46032
317/844-6125

For Pet's Sake offers professional pet grooming at reasonable rates. Pamper your pet with their thorough shampooing and brushing, nail cutting, and ear cleaning. Bring on the bows to complete the, *voila'*, metamorphosis of the canine customer.

HUMANE SOCIETY OF INDY
7929 N. Michigan
Indianapolis, IN 46268
317/872-5650

Why not save a life and give a home to a homeless dog or cat? There are sensible restrictions. They'll have to interview you to make sure the pet you are adopting is a good match for you and your family. Then it's up to you to give all the love you can to your newest member of the family. Animals have been thoroughly examined, given their shots and neutered or spayed.

PET SUPPLIES PLUS
7190 Rockville Rd.
Indianapolis, IN 46214
317/241-1400

Dog food, cat food, leashes...the list goes on and on. Get 'em all at discounted prices.

PETSMART
8251 US 31 S.
Indianapolis, IN 46227
317/888-5325

Where can you take your pet shopping? Petsmart allows your furry friends, as long as you keep them on a leash. They guarantee the lowest prices over 9,000 items. So whatever Rover must have, Rover can get...and claim his own savings too.
Additional Locations: 2238 Broadripple Ave. 317/475-9603
4072 Pendleton Way 317/549-9229

SPECK'S PET SUPPLY

12669 Rockville Rd.
Indianapolis, IN 46234
317/272-7738

Not only does Speck's carry a large selection of feed & supplies, the facility offers a shot clinic, and a do-it-yourself flea dip all at deep savings.
Additional Locations: 1625 W. Smith Valley Rd. Ste 3-E 317/889-6738
12669 Rockville Rd. 317/272-7738

TOP DOG PET SUPPLIES

7844 N. Michigan
Indianapolis, IN 46268
317/876-0061

Three cheers for the top dog—Hip - Hip…Hooray! Save on pet food & supplies for all pets. Unless your pet happens to be the rare Albino Snoozit. Then it depends…do they eat dog food? At any rate, come here for a large selection and low prices.
Additional Locations: 7858 E. 96th St., Fishers 317/578-4443
11594 Westfield Blvd., Carmel 317/844-7266

PHOTO LABS & STUDIOS

BEST BUYS

9977 E. Washington
Indianapolis, IN
317/897-3941

Get double 35mm prints of 3 1/2 in. by 5in., 24 exposures, for under $4.00. 4 in. by 6 in. prints of 24 exposures is under $6.00.
Additional Location: 5820 E. 82nd St. 317/841-0711
5402 W. 38th 317/290-1330

MASTER LAB

9713 E. Washington
Indianapolis, IN 46229
317/898-4161

Shoot! Had you only remembered to have the children's picture taken three weeks ago, it would have made a perfect gift for your parents...It's not too late! Master Lab will do quality portrait packages in about an hour. All ages are welcome and packages are available in black and white or color.

PHAR-MOR

8800 US 31 S.
Indianapolis, IN 46227
317/889-1159

Phar-Mor offers a free roll of film with their specials! Ask about their low price guarantee on prescriptions. Here you can save on everything from prescriptions to health and beauty needs and they also have video rental for 98¢ for two nights. Or, you can rent three videos for around $2.50 for two nights. You can't beat that price for a couple of nights of entertainment.
Additional Locations: 10235 E. Washington 317/897-1159
Lafayette Place 317/293-6175
Castleton Plaza 317/841-0393

ROBERTS DISTRIBUTORS
225 S. Meridian
Indianapolis, IN 46225
317/636-5544

Roberts' lets you custom crop your special photo the way you want it. They also have the latest photography equipment at competitive prices. If the cutting edge of technology isn't your speed, they also have a large selection of new and used 35mm cameras which take very sharp picture. Rentals are available and trade-ins are welcomed.

TARGET
8101 E. Washington
Indianapolis, IN
317/898-3636

Economize double 35mm prints for $3.99! If they're dropped off before the posted date one day, they're returned the very next day. Target's photo department has several sizes and film formats, not to mention their great selection of photo gifts including puzzles, mugs, ornaments and more.

WAL-MART
7245 US 31 S.
Indianapolis, IN 46227
317/888-7906

For either one-hour photos or regular delivery check the prices at Wal-Mart. The one-hour prices can't be beat! Most locations have a photo studio that has specials often costing under $10.00.

PLANTS, LAWN & GARDEN

THE FOUNTAIN FACTORY
4949 W. 96th
Indianapolis, IN 46268
317/872-9555

The Fountain Factory has bird baths, flower pots and, yes, fountains for less. Increase the curb appeal of your home by an immeasurable amount with the purchase of a few relatively inexpensive, yet beautiful landscaping pieces.

QUALITY STONE
St. Rd. 38 East
Noblesville, IN 46060
317/773-5597

Stone from 37 states delivered to wherever you want. Do you like the look of stone, but don't know exactly what to do with it? The staff at Quality Stone will help you choose beautiful, yet economical, projects. They have a complete selection including patio, walk, veneer, flag, and landscaping stones and more.

STONE CENTER OF INDIANA
5272 E. 65th St.
Indianapolis, IN 46220
317/849-9100
800/300-3197

Fireplace stone, used brick, flagstone, sand retaining stones, and pebbles are only a small sample of what you will find at the Stone Center. Their friendly staff is more than happy to give advice and consultation as part of their service—for no extra charge! They also have statuary to put the finishing touch on your landscape.

SCHUSTER'S BLOCK, INC.
901 E. Troy Ave.
Indianapolis, IN 46203
317/787-3201

For all your brick and block needs for building and patio, Schuster's Block, Inc. has been serving Central Indiana since 1918. They have a large inventory of face brick, concrete and clay pavers, patio brick and more. Stop by and see their display to help you determine your needs. They're always open Monday through Friday and Saturdays hours are seasonal.

≺ NURSERIES ≻

RISCH GREENHOUSE
5540 S. Meridian
Indianapolis, IN 46217
317/787-4769

Whether it's the red or blue flowers of delicate columbine or the dependable blooms of yarrow you yearn for, adding a little bloom in your life doesn't have to be expensive. Flower bedding is in these days and Risch's can help you make a floral splash for less. They also sell a variety of other goods, all at competitive prices.

STOUT'S FLORIST & GREENHOUSE
5245 Bluff Rd.
Indianapolis, IN 46217
317/786-1479

Shhh...mum's the word. Or "geraniums" depending on what time of the year it is. Retail and wholesale flowers, plants and other landscaping needs for far less than you would expect to pay! They're also very affordable on cut flowers: a dozen roses is only $35.00 plus delivery.

TIFFANY LAWN & GARDEN SUPPLY INC. *

940 E. Michigan
Indianapolis, IN 46202
317/638-3405

Saving 10 to 50% on landscaping is a snap at Tiffany's. Since 1979, they have been selling quality landscaping goods, like grass seed, stepping stones, treated timbers, fertilizers, soils and more. Weed-X landscape fabric is only $9.72 for a 3 ft. by 50 ft. roll. Their everyday low price on white marble chips is $2.77 and bulk mulch is their specialty. The list of savings goes on and on. They sell and manufacturer bulk and bagged landscape products, then they sell them wholesale—to the public! Is the reason you keep putting off the project because you don't have time to pick up your supplies? That's not a good excuse; they'll deliver. Volume discounts are available and Mastercard and Visa are accepted.

POOL & PATIO

≺ BARBECUES ≻

ALLIED APPLIANCE CO.
8901 Southeastern
Indianapolis, IN 46239
317/862-6653

Don't throw the old rooster roaster out! It can be repaired. In fact, you can probably do it yourself with parts from Allied. Allied carries parts for all makes and models. If you are ready for a dependable and easy gas grill, they can still help you with their large selection. They even fill natural gas and propane tanks, too.

≺ PATIO FURNITURE ≻

THE DECK & PATIO SHOP
6125 Southeastern
Indianapolis, IN 462
317/356-9535

"The largest casual furniture store in Indiana." You won't believe your choice of groupings. Choose from wooden, wrought iron, wicker, or rattan. They are open seven days a week. Call for off-season hours. MasterCard and Visa are accepted.

≺ POOL SUPPLIES ≻

LESLIE'S SWIMMING POOL SUPPLIES
7211 N. Keystone Ave.
Indianapolis, IN 462
317/257-7911

"We will not be undersold." That pretty much sums it up. That does leave out a couple of things...like their free water testing, free labor on most in-store repairs, and their large selection of chemicals, equipment, toys and accessories.

POOL CITY

3826 Georgetown Rd.
Indianapolis, IN 46254
317/297-3612

Very competitive prices on pool supplies, accessories and even the pool itself. Pool City also sells spas and fireplaces and has a large selection and a very knowledgeable sales staff. If you're having trouble getting your chemicals just right, ask them for advice. They're almost always able to help you solve your problem.

≺ SPAS ≻

FIREPLACE PATIO & SPA CENTER

5678 Crawfordsville Rd.
Indianapolis, IN 46214
317/243-3259

Discount prices on portable and inground spas, chemicals and accessories. Fireplaces are discounted, too. Need something to put under that hot tub? They sell custom designed decks.

HOT TUBS PLUS

200 W. Smith Valley Rd.
Greenwood, IN 46142
317/888-6222

Who can pass up factory-direct prices from the hot water professionals. Hot Tubs Plus can help you with your hot tub dreams with a custom spas made to your specifications. They can work to create custom spas to your specifications. Hot Tubs Plus can design a hot tub heaven in your back yard at factory direct prices.

ROYAL SPA

2041 W. Epler
Indianapolis, IN 46217
317/781-0828
800/541-1248

Luxurious spas made in Indiana, so you don't have to pay the shipping costs, directly or indirectly. Royal has a very large selection of colors and styles available. Their selection of parts is unbeatable. We recently searched the town over for a part that no one else had. Actually, it was a part for a spa that their competitor sells. Royal Spa didn't hold it against us, though, and found just the part we needed.

WATSON'S

11801 Pendleton Pike
Oaklandon, IN 46236
317/823-4448

"One of the largest selections in the Midwest," selling pools, spas, supplies, and accessories. Watson's is a common name in Central Indiana—with uncommon prices.

RECYCLING

INDIANAPOLIS RECYCLES

317/327-7000

Indianapolis Recycles is sponsored by the Clean City Committee of the Department of Public Works. Who else would be better to keep the public informed on locations, materials accepted, and more.

INDY RECYCLING

6933 E. 42nd
Indianapolis, IN 46226
317/545-8888

Indy Recycling accepts the most common recyclable items plus copper, brass, magazines/catalogues, and plastic (1,2,3,6). "Indy's one-stop recycling center." Just drive up and recycle.

RUMPKE

800/821-6095

Whether you want to recycle at home or at the office, Rumpke has a service for you. They can do a free waste audit on site to evaluate your company's needs and create a customized plan. Not only do they deal with commercial and residential recycling; they also service church and civic group drives.

SECURITY, SAFES & VAULTS

≺ SAFES & VAULTS ≻

CARMEL LOCK & SAFE CO.

20 8th St. NW
Carmel, IN 46032
317/896-9103

Choose from a large selection of competitively priced new and used safes for every possible need. No need to panic if you can't remember how to get back in your car or home, their mobile company, A Arsenal, has 24 hour emergency service. Just call 317/631-7233.

BOB'S SAFE LOCK & KEY SERVICE, INC.

5631 S. Madison Ave.
Indianapolis, IN 46227
317/783-3861

Ever notice the stickers by the lock on merchants doors? Start paying attention and you'll be amazed how many of them say "Bob's Lock." They also serve residential customers and can even change the combination for you on an existing safe.

ROBERTSON SAFE & LOCK SERVICE

209 S. Bridgeport Rd.
Indianapolis, IN 46231
317/271-9078

"A safe man to call..." Since 1948. Robertson has been doing business and saving you money on new and used safes.

≺ SECURITY SYSTEMS ≻

CIRCLE CITY ALARM & SECURITY SYSTEMS

5355 E. 38th
Indpls. IN 46218
317/542-7087

Whether you want to buy or just lease a security system, check into Circle City Alarm "before you pay too much" someplace else. Circle City offers quality service at affordable prices. Systems are available with or without monitoring.

INDY ELECTRONICS

4374 Madison Ave.
Indianapolis, IN 46227
317/786-4646

Your stereo is broken and you're unable to listen to the weekly top ten list! Indy Electronics wants you to look to them to solve the problem.. You'll find name brands such as Pioneer, Sony, Panasonic, and Pyle. They'll meet or beat all competitors' prices and do the installation for you. While you're there, check out their great prices on alarms, CBs, and radar detectors.

SHOES

≺ FAMILY ≻

HUSH PUPPIES

11626 N. E. Executive Dr.
Edinburgh, IN 46124
812/526-0291

Save money on kids' footwear? You betcha. In fact, you can save 20 to 50% on footwear for the whole family! Town & Country, Brooks, Wimzees, Hush Puppies and more can be found here.
Additional Locations: Horizon Outlet Center, Fremont 219/833-1026
Lighthouse Place, Michigan City 219/872-0809

SAM'S NAME BRAND SHOES & ACCESSORIES

5205 E. 38th
Indianapolis, IN 46218
317/546-7267

We can't mention the brands by name, but we can tell you they're all recognizable and they're sold at discount prices. They have a large selection to complete any wardrobe.

SHOE CARNIVAL/CARNIVAL SHOES

10203 E. Washington
Indianapolis, IN 46229
317/895-2400

Why pay $49.99 for the very same shoe that sells elsewhere for $39.99? When asked what brands they carry, Shoe Carnival will tell you, "All name brands." For savings on shoes under $20.00, spin their savings wheel to determine your own discounts.
Additional locations: 7799 U.S. 31 S. 317/887-3865
3717 Commercial Dr. 317/291-6242
599 Westfield, Noblesville 317/776-6740
6316 E. 82nd 317/845-8490

STOUT'S SHOES

318 Massachusetts Ave.
Indianapolis, IN 46204
317/632-7818

Heads up! In our opinion, it should be a prerequisite for an Indiana high school diploma that each student visit the downtown Stout's location so that he or she can appreciate the ingenuity of merchants from years gone by. Here, the inventory is kept upstairs and instead of running up and downstairs for shoes, they are simply conveyed down a wire pulley system in a basket. If they don't suit or don't fit—back up they go. As amusing as it is, it's not the only reason to visit them. Stout's also has the state's largest selection of hard-to-fit sizes—ranging from 5 1/2 to 18 and AA to EEE in men's and from 3 1/2 to 14 and AAAAA to EE in women's. Children's sizes are available too.
Additional locations: 13155 N. Meridian 317/848-5432
7249 U.S. 31 S. 317/889-6715

< MEN'S >

FLORSHEIM SHOES

11626 N. E. Executive Dr.
Edinburgh, IN 46124
812/526-5528

Save 50% to 75% on first-quality, close-outs and irregulars. These popular men's shoes come direct from the factory in a selection of athletic, casual and dress. Worried they won't have your size? Is it somewhere between a 6 and a 15? Between A and EEE? Yes? Then there's no need to worry. They have selections in all of those sizes.
Additional Locations: Horizon Outlet Center, Fremont 219/833-6244

≺ MEN'S & WOMEN'S ≻

9 WEST

601 Wabash St.
Michigan City, IN 46360
219/872-1655

We found a great pair of shoes whose regular retail price was $56.00 for $39.00. Many pairs were 50% off and savings on clearance merchandise were even greater. They have men's and women's shoes in the very latest styles for less. Major credit cards are accepted.

BANISTER SHOES

11626 N. E. Executive Dr.
Edinburgh, IN 46124
812/526-9721

Women's and men's casual and athletic shoes for up to 50%. Brands include Capezio, Liz Claiborne and scores more.
Additional Locations: Horizon Outlet Center, Fremont 219/833-1026
Lighthouse Place, Michigan City 219/872-0809

BARGIN BOB SHOES

489 S. State Rd. 135
Greenwood, IN 46143
317/881-8013

A shoe for all occasions. Bargin Bob's sells famous make and designer label shoes for 40 to 70% less than suggested retail! They've been dealing in discounted, quality men's and women's footwear for over three decades and have it down to an artform. You'll be amazed at the selection of styles and sizes for both men and women with savings that can't be beat. Inventory is constantly updated, so visit frequently!

BASS SHOES
11626 N. E. Executive Dr.
Edinburgh, IN 46124
812/526-5902

Save 25% or more on first quality leather shoes for men and women. Lines include Bucs, Weejuns, Sunjuns, and more. They also sell accessories at great savings.
Additional Locations: Horizon Outlet Center, Fremont 219/833-1026
Lighthouse Place, Michigan City 219/872-0809

BOOT FACTORY
601 Wabash St.
Michigan City, IN 46360
219/874-0291

Overruns, imperfects, closeouts, and first-quality boots line the shelves here. Save on famous brands, like Laredo, for men and women.

DESIGNER SHOE WAREHOUSE
8510 Center Run Dr.
Indianapolis, IN 46250
317/594-0069

With over 30,000 name brand and designer name men's and women's shoes, Designer Shoe Warehouse claims the largest selection in the city. More than 900 styles and over 165 brand names are in stock. We're not permitted to mention the brand names they stock; however, they're the same as found in all the top department stores! They close every Tuesday and Wednesday to restock with thousands of new pairs, so it's like shopping a new shoe store each week!

GREAT WESTERN BOOT CO.

9455 Haver Way
Indianapolis, IN 46240
317/848-1020

"Great selection! Great Prices!" Over 10,000 pairs of boots are in stock here including famous manufacturers like Dingo, Tony Lama, and Stetson. They accept "Mastercard, Visa, American Express, Discover, Cash, Check, or Gold Dust."

EL-BEE SHOE OUTLET

1300 E. 86th St.
Indianapolis, IN 46240
317/848-4029

You'll experience savings of 15 to 60% off comparable retail on athletic shoes like Nike and Reebok, and casual shoes like Dingo, Hush Puppies and Papagallo. Plus many more brands in lots of styles and sizes.
Additional locations: Several throughout Indiana

FAMOUS FOOTWEAR

7150 E Washington
Indianapolis, IN 46219
317/356-5513

Check out their low price guarantee. They guarantee savings of about 10 to 50% on all your footwear needs, including dress, athletic, and casual. They have styles and sizes for the entire family.

≺ WOMEN'S ≻

ETIENNE AIGNER

601 Wabash St.
Michigan City, IN 46360
219/879-0318

Aigner for 30% below retail for designer footwear? It's not a misprint!

NICKELS
601 Wabash St.
Michigan City, IN 46360
219/872-6848

A large selection of competitively priced footwear and accessories for women, with a variety of sizes and styles available.

< WORK SHOES & BOOTS >

GILVIN'S WORK BOOTS & SHOES
3838 Madison Ave.
Indianapolis, IN 46227
317/783-3210

Ever wondered where to buy steel-toed boots? You can get them, and get them for less, too. Gilvin's has competitive prices on a variety of work boots and shoes for men and women—in fact, they have one of the largest selections in the state! Brands include Carolina, Wolverine, Knapp and more. If you're hard to fit, don't despair, they can special order.

HOOSIER SAFETY FOOTWEAR INC.
5960 E. 25th
Indianapolis, IN 46218
317/547-3338

Friendly, personal service at prices that are very competitive, whether you are looking for steel-toed boots, moccasins, pumps, hiking boots, or any other style. Check out their prices before you buy. They have men's and women's sizes in a variety of styles.

SPORTS & RECREATION

≺ BICYCLES ≻

BARGAIN BICYCLES

6001 S. US 31
Whiteland, IN 46184
317/535-7607

Trying to get back into shape? What better way to do it than bicycling? Bargain Bicycles has many kinds of bicycles in all price ranges. Whether you're looking for a new bike, or want to save even more by buying a used one, you'll want to survey the selection of more than 125 bicycles for less than what you would pay at a sporting goods store. All of their used bicycles are have been inspected to make sure they are safe and dependable.

MATTHEW'S BICYCLE MART INC.

7272 Pendleton Pike
Indianapolis, IN 46226
317/547-3456

If cycling is your way to keep fit or you just do it for enjoyment, Matthew's Bicycle Mart, Inc. offers low prices by stocking with last year's models at close-out prices. They carry everything from cross bikes to tandems, 2,000 bicycles in all! Layaway and financing are available.

≺ EXERCISE EQUIPMENT ≻

BOB BLOCK
8128 Castleton Ct. W.
Indianapolis, IN 46250
317/845-7700

Where else can you buy exercise equipment from a store-owner with a Doctorate in physical education and a former college coach? Bob Block's has more than 10,000 square feet of aerobic and strength/conditioning equipment at the "best prices" in town. Part of every great fitness routine is healthy relaxation. Bob also carries cedar and redwood saunas and steam mist shower units. On any equipment a customer purchases, they provide free on-site setup and training.

FITNESS WAREHOUSE
8014 S. US 31
Indianapolis, IN 46227
317/882-2300

Fitness Warehouse guarantees the lowest prices around on their large selection of treadmills, stairclimbers, lifecycles, skiers and more. Financing is available and all purchases are guaranteed for one full year or more.

≺ GAME ROOM ≻

A-1 BILLIARDS & TROPHY
1209 E. 46
Indianapolis, IN 46236
317/255-8682

Anyone for a game of pool? A-1 Billiards & Trophy can set you up with one of their new, used, or antique pool tables. They will buy, sell or move your existing table. If you're only interested in a Brunswick, check our their great prices.

< GOLF >

THE GOLF OUTLET

11626 N. E. Executive Dr.
Edinburgh, IN 46124
812/526-9506

A full line of clubs and accessories with a total of 15 brand names. Save up to 20% on brands like: Wilson, Top-Flite, Peerless, Ram, Knight, Reebok, and Dexter. Major credit cards, layaway, checks, and in-store financing are all available. You may save enough money to support your green fees for awhile.

NEVADA BOB'S DISCOUNT GOLF

832 U.S. 31 N.
Greenwood, IN 46142
317/881-4121

New clubs for your trip around the links at bargain prices are available at the "world's largest chain of discount golf shops." Nevada Bob's carries all major brands at discount prices; they buy direct and save. If you need to practice on that swing this winter, use Nevada Bob's indoor putting and driving range.
Additional Location: 5516 E. 82nd St. 317/595-0008

PRO GOLF DISCOUNT

275 S. State Rd. 135
Greenwood, IN 46142
317/888-3010

Just what every major golf enthusiast wants—a complete line of major brand golf equipment and accessories at discount prices. Pro Golf is able to offer such great prices due to their 190-store buying power. In fact, they are so sure they can beat your best price on any piece of equipment in stock, they will give you that equipment free if they can't. Wow! How's that for beating the competitor?
Additional locations: 3489 W. 86th St. 317/879-8783
10015 E. Washington St. 317/895-0127

5190 Pike Plaza Rd. 317/299-7019
8326 Castleton Corner Dr. 317/841-7513

SUPREME GOLF

2310 E. 146th
Carmel, IN 46032
317/846-4653

Ever wanted to get the clubs out and sink a few birdies—in the two feet of snow that's on the ground? Let your frustration end—Supreme Golf is open year-round, so you can use their driving ranges. And if you are in the market for a new set of clubs, you'll be glad to hear of their "Never Undersold Price Guarantee."

≺ GUNS & AMMO ≻

DON'S GUNS

736 Lows Blvd.
Greenwood, IN 46142
317/882-4867

Choose from a variety of guns and try them out in the indoor shooting range at Don's. If it's not a gun you're interested in, browse through their fishing tackle and live bait. They are open seven days a week and offer in-store financing.
Additional locations: 96th & Keystone 317/574-0800
3807 Lafayette Rd. 317/297-4242

SACKS EAGLE LOAN CO.

317 N. Delaware
Indianapolis, IN 46204
317/635-6556

If you're looking for that hard-to-find gun, try Sacks Eagle Loan Co. They carry a large selection of competitively-priced guns, specializing in the hard-to-find rifles, shotguns, and handguns. Save even more money by taking advantage of their daily public sales.

WINDSOR GUNS, INC.

4027 S. Franklin Rd.
Indianapolis, IN 46239
317/862-2512

From the avid collector to the squirrel hunter, you'll find what you need at Windsor Guns, Inc. They buy, sell, and trade new and used guns and carry everything from handguns to muzzelloaders with complete gunsmithing service offered.

< SPORTING GOODS & OTHER SPORTS >

FALL CREEK BAIT & TACKLE

4215 E. Fall Creek Pkwy. N. Dr.
Indianapolis, IN 46205
317/251-9229

The kids are in the car, fishing tackle in the back, reservations made. What else could you need...Bait! On your way, stop by Fall Creek Bait & Tackle. They are open seven days a week and carry a complete line of bait and tackle. When you catch that 40-pound walleye, put it on ice and let Fall Creek Bait & Tackle preserve it for you with their taxidermy service. If archery is your sport, they offer complete arrow sales and repairs. Join one of their Target & Bow Hunter leagues and practice in their indoor range.

J & J ARCHERY

3438 Madison Ave.
Indianapolis, IN 46227
317/784-3632

Factory-trained technicians are featured at J & J Archery. The facility not only provides sales and service, but also arrow-fletching and repair and mossy oak clothing at competitive prices. They also have leagues for men, women, and teens in their large indoor range.

— *RESALE* —

PLAY IT AGAIN SPORTS

1955 E. Stop 13
Indianapolis, IN 46227
317/889-9978

Save up to 50% off original prices of sporting goods. A wide variety of equipment for golf, skiing, and team sports. Groups, and leagues, can save an additional 20%. Most major credit cards are accepted and layaway is available.
Additional Locations: Speedway Plaza 317/481-9750, 9455 E. Washington 317/897-4020, 2152 E. 116th 317/848-1815

SECOND TIME AROUND SPORTS

4939 S. Emerson
Indianapolis, IN 46203
317/781-6813

If high prices have kept you from purchasing that stairstepper or ski machine, wait no more. Second Time Around Sports offers terrific prices on new and recycled exercise equipment and sporting goods. If you're tired of using the same piece of equipment, trade it in! Second Time not only sells, but they will buy, trade, or sell on consignment.

SPORTS TRADERS

5753 E. 86th
Indianapolis, IN 46250
317/842-4812

Since 1992, Sports Traders has been saving Hoosiers 20 to 70% on used and new sporting goods. They buy, sell, and trade equipment for fitness, weight lifting, golf, soccer, skiing, football, baseball, hockey, and many other sports. Mastercard, Visa, Discover, and personal checks are accepted. In-store financing is also available.
Additional Location: 55 S. State 317/842-4812

≺ TRAVEL NEEDS ≻

AMERICAN TOURISTER
11626 N. E. Executive Dr.
Edinburgh, IN 46124
812/526-0051

You can save from 40% to 70% off high-quality luggage and travel-related products. Items include soft and hard-sided luggage, sports bags, and attaché cases. Shipping is available in the continental U.S.
Additional Locations: Lighthouse Place 219/879-6730

SURPLUS & SALVAGE

ANGELO'S INC.

201 S. College
Indianapolis, IN 46202
317/634-6552

Have you ever wondered what happens to the stuff in the back of the semi that's on its side on the shoulder of the road? More than likely, the insurance company settles with the owner of the goods and then they sell the goods to someplace like Angelo's for pennies on the dollar. Angelo's then passes the savings on to you. This means you get perfectly good, although possibly dented, saleables such as canned goods and other items for up to 50% or more off their regular selling price.

ARMY & NAVY SURPLUS OUTLETS INC.

1702 E. Washington
Indianapolis, IN 46201
317/636-2787

"You're in the army now..." or out...it doesn't really matter—Army & Navy Surplus has something for everyone. You can choose from their large selection of fatigues, T-shirts, jackets, and other goods. You can even have dog tags custom made. They're open six days a week for your convenience.
Additional Location: 2989 W. 71st 317/293-3213

ARMY-NAVY INDIANAPOLIS SURPLUS STORE

6032 E. 21st
Indianapolis, IN 46219
317/356-0856

Before you go to the local sporting goods store and spend a fortune to get ready for your camping excursion, make a trip to the Army-Navy Surplus Store. They have wilderness goods and camping supplies here that cost as little as half of what they do at your regular camping goods store. They also sell military clothing for just about everyone.

SURPLUS BARGAIN CENTER
2611 W. Michigan
Indianapolis, IN 46222
317/637-8513

Is it Army softgoods you're looking for? Surplus Bargain Center has a large assortment of surplus military clothing in a large assortment of styles and colors, in addition to many other military items.

THINGS TO DO

ARTCRAFT THEATRE

57 N. Main
Franklin, IN 46131
317/736-6337

The Artcraft Theatre shows first-run movies daily at huge savings. Before 6:00 all tickets are only $2.00 each and after 6:00 an adult ticket is $3.00 and tickets for children are only $2.00.

THE CHILDREN'S MUSEUM

3000 N. Meridian
Indianapolis, IN 46208
317/924-5437
800/208-KIDS

Indy is fortunate enough to be the home of the world's largest children's museum. The best part is, the children can do more than just look at the exhibits here. Several activity areas are set up throughout the museum to teach children of all ages about different aspects of the world we live and you'll find everything from archeological digs, playing different musical instruments from around the world, to playing in the water and sand! Youth tickets, for ages 2 through 17, are only $3.00 and adult tickets are $6.00. On Thursdays they have extended hours and from 5:00 to 8:00 admission is free. An annual family pass is available for $25.00, which not only provides admission for the entire family, but also allows for discounts on purchases at the museum.

CINEMARK MOVIES 8
10445 E. Washington
Indianapolis, IN 46229
317/898-1990

Cinemark has eight theaters showing current and popular movies. All tickets are $1.50 for all shows, except on Tuesdays when tickets are only $1.00.

STATE PARKS DEPARTMENT
612 State Office Building
Indianapolis, IN 46204
317/232-4124

The State Parks Department provides a wealth of information about state parks and activities. They also sell state park passes for $18.00 for the whole calendar year.

DIAL A MOVIE
1400 N. Meridian Suite 201
Indianapolis, IN 46202
317/634-3800

Are you worried that your child will see something unsuitable for his age at the movies? The National Catholic Office provides an information line on which they provide information about movies they have rated. Their categories include A1, suitable for the entire family, A2, suitable for teenagers, A3, suitable for adults, A4, not suitable for those with moral objections, and O, morally offensive for all ages.

INDIANAPOLIS INDIANS
1501 W. 16th
Indianapolis, IN 46202
317/269-3545

"Take me out to the ball game..." and in Indianapolis it won't cost you a fortune. Tickets are available in a variety of coupon books for savings of about 25 to 40%. The best value of all is for kids. Children aged 14 and under can join the Knot Hole Club for $7.00. This entitles them to admission to all regular home games and a Pepsi T-shirt. And, of course, season tickets are available.

INDIANAPOLIS MUSEUM OF ART

1200 W. 38th
Indianapolis, IN 46208
317/920-2660

Educational, entertaining and free...you just can't beat that combination. There is never a charge for their permanent collection and the charge to non-members for special exhibits never exceeds $7.00 per family. On Thursdays, even the special exhibits are free.

INDIANAPOLIS SYMPHONY ORCHESTRA

45 Monument Circle
Indianapolis, IN 46204
317/639-4300

Call the box office for information on scheduled noon-time concerts that are free to the community. The concerts usually last about an hour and it's interesting to see the spectrum of different people there—everyone from businesswomen and men to housewives with children. This is a great way to expose your children to classical music without having to worry about short attention spans. Then you can buy season tickets for their evening concerts and for the whole family to enjoy.

INDIANAPOLIS ZOO

1200 W. Washington
Indianapolis, IN 46222
317/630-2030

On the first Tuesday of each month the zoo has "Community morning." From 9:00 until noon, admission is only $3.00 and children under two get free admission. There is also no charge for parking at that time. If you plan on visiting the zoo frequently, they have a variety of annual passes available. An individual annual pass is $35.00, a pass for an individual with one guest is $40.00 and a family pass is $50.00. If you think you might want an annual pass, but aren't quite sure, visit the zoo and pay regular admission and then if you decide you want one, the zoo will apply that day's admission towards the purchase of an annual pass.

INDY PARKS & RECREATION ACTIVITY LINE
"Fun Guide"
317/327-0000

There's no excuse for boredom if you've called the Indy Parks & Recreation Activity Line. They will supply you with information on 6,000 things to do around town! Activities include public swimming, golfing, plays and more.

THE IRVING
5507 E. Washington
Indianapolis, IN 46219
317/357-3792

Admission ranges from 99¢ to $4.00 in this historic theatre in venerable Irvington. Seniors and college students can receive additional discounts. Call for their current list of movies and show times.

LEAPS AND BOUNDS
3720 E. 82nd
Indianapolis, IN 46240
317/577-1565

This is a great rainy day activity, or any other day for that matter. Leaps and Bounds is a playcenter with all sorts of physical activities for children, a great way for them to get rid of pent-up energy in a safe environment. The equipment is designed for safety; in fact the whole set-up is designed for safety—they have a special child-parent matching system to help insure that a child leaves only with the person he came with. They offer special admission prices through the week and group packages are available. They also have private after-hour programs for groups.

OLD INDIANA FUN PARK

7230 350 West
Thorntown, IN 46071
317/873-4141

Old Indiana offers unlimited use of over 30 amusements rides as well as live entertainment with singing, dancing, and animal shows. The park just completed its all new Splash Mountain Waterline and water activity area with seven different slides ranging from mild to wild. For the younger crowd they have a baby pool and giant sand box. Watch for their special promotions and coupons for savings on single visit tickets or you can purchase a season pass and come as many times as you like.

PUBLIC LIBRARY FILM SERIES

40 E. St. Clair St.
Indianapolis, IN 46204
317/269-1772

On Sundays the Marion County Public Library offers a film series covering a variety of topics and interests to the public free of charge. Call for more information and the series schedule.

WENS FLICK CLUB

950 N. Meridian
Indianapolis, IN 46204
317/266-9700
Fax: 317/634-1618

Approximately 300 pairs of tickets per movie premier are available to the members in the WENS Flick Club. To join, send your name, address, telephone number, and age to the above address or you can fax it to the above fax number. You will be notified when it's your turn for tickets.

WZPL MOVIE CLUB

1440 N. Meridian St.
Indianapolis, IN 46202
317/637-8000
317/263-2533

Free movie passes are given to members by mail. The tickets are offered round robin. Currently members are receiving tickets about four times a year, but that can change based on the number of people that join. To join, write or fax your name and address.

VARIETY STORES

BIG LOTS
4711 W. 30th
Indianapolis, IN 46222
317/291-6082

Big lots, odd lots, buy-outs, overstocks, and discontinued lines characterize Big Lots operation. Clothing, toys, decorations, picture frames, and even some furniture. All this and more at steeply discounted prices. In addition to their everyday low prices, there are weekly specials. Check out the circulars for even more savings.
Additional Locations: 3415 English Ave. 317/635-2743
7299 N. Keystone 317/251-4905
5520 Madison Ave. 317/782-0165
8939 E. 38th 317/846-7961

≺ ONE DOLLAR STORES ≻

$1 SHOP
7307 US 31 S
Indianapolis, IN 46227
317/865-9540

Who says $1.00 won't buy anything anymore? At the $1 Shop it can buy a record, tape, necklace, decorative piece, or any of several other surprises.

ALL FOR ONE
3479 W. 86th
Indianapolis, IN 46268
317/876-9565

Give the children a real treat. There's nothing like getting a dollar and going to a store where you can pick out anything you want, and this is the place to do that. Choose from their selection of toys, housewares, snack items, garage items, and other wonderful "treasures." They're

known for their selection of Mylar balloons (including helium) for one dollar. Your kids will thank you—just don't forget the nickel for tax!
Additional Locations: 7150 E. Washington 317/353-6282
3639 Commercial Dr. 317/291-4007
Southern Plaza 317/782-8064
5824 Crawfordsville Rd. 317/243-2474

DOLLAR TREE

Greenwood Place
Indianapolis, IN 46227
317/881-7162

A friendly store with aisles and aisles of bargains that are only a dollar each! Holiday decorations, household goods, and toys are among the thousands of items in their large inventory.
Additional Locations: Nora Plaza 317/580-9563
Village Park Plaza 317/846-8931

IT'S REALLY $1

3749 Commercial Dr.
Indianapolis, IN 46222
317/293-3316

Another place to stretch a buck. Get all of your party paper goods at great discounts. They also sell household goods, candy and snacks, health and beauty needs, toys, costume jewelry, hair ribbons and more. You won't believe what you can get for one dollar!
Additional Locations: 7673 Shelby 317/8814555
5868 E. 82nd 317/841-1310

IV
Directory
of
Outlet Malls

NOTE

Descriptions of most stores are included in the appropriate category in the DIRECTORY OF STORES portion of the book. The following lists the current directory of all stores (except stores that requested to be excluded) that are located at the site, regardless of whether or not they are manufacturer outlets. While most are discount locations, there are a few specialty shops that do not discount merchandise below "retail."

Due to the popularity of discount shopping, many of the listed malls are undergoing expansion which means constant changes in their directories. Call the information center for each mall and request a copy of the current directory. If you are making the trip for a particular outlet, we suggest calling ahead to make sure they are still in business and located in the same place.

EDINBURGH

HORIZON OUTLET CENTER

US-31 and I-65, Exit 76B
Edinburgh, IN 46124
(800) 866-5900
(812) 526-9764
HOURS: Mon.-Sat. 9a.m.-8p.m., Sun. 11a.m.-6p.m.

AILEEN STORES	812/526-2780
AMERICAN TOURISTER	812/526-0051
BANISTER SHOES	812/526-9721
BARBIZON	812/526-5958
BASS SHOE	812/526-5902
BIG CHILL	812/526-0208
BLACK & DECKER	812/526-8321
BON WORTH FACTORY STORE	812/526-8386
BOOK WAREHOUSE	812/526-9860
BRASS FACTORY	812/526-6281
BUGLE BOY	812/526-0771

CAPE ISLE KNITTERS	812/526-6882
CHAMPION HANES	812/526-2592
CORNING/REVERE FACTORY STORE	812/526-2678
COUNTRY SOURCE	812/526-8214
FACTORY BRAND SHOES	NEW
FAMOUS BRANDS HOUSEWARES	812/526-8872
FANNY FARMER	812/526-5933
FARAH FACTORY STORE	812/526-9500
FARBERWARE	812/526-0025
FIELDCREST CANNON	812/526-2887
FLORSHEIM SHOE	812/526-5528
HUSH PUPPIES FACTORY DIRECT	812/526-0291
IZOD FACTORY STORE	812/526-6954
JONATHAN LOGAN	812/526-8210
KITCHEN COLLECTION	812/526-9518
L'EGGS HANES BALI	812/526-6391
LEATHER LOFT	812/526-2366
LESLIE FAY	812/526-0331
LEVI'S OUTLET BY DESIGNS	812/526-9644
MAIDENFORM	812/526-9570
NOT JUST POPCORN	812/526-8256
PAPER FACTORY	812/526-5096
PEPPERIDGE FARM	812/526-8941
PERFUMANIA	812/526-9789
PRESTIGE FRAGRANCE & COSMETICS	812/526-9049
SANDWICHES, ETC.	812/526-9390
SARA LEE OUTLET	812/526-6890
SOCK GALORE	812/526-2422
SPIEGEL	NEW
STONE MOUNTAIN HANDBAGS	812/526-8110
SWANK	812/526-2800
SWEATSHIRT COMPANY	812/526-0545
THE GOLF OUTLET	812/526-9506
TOOL WAREHOUSE	812/526-5298
TOY LIQUIDATORS	812/526-6838
VAN HEUSEN	812/526-6220

WELCOME HOME	812/526-5760
WESTPORT, LTD.	812/526-0131
WINDSOR SHIRT COMPANY	812/526-0355
WOODEN BENCH	812/526-8180
ZAK'S CONFECTIONS	812/526-8306

FREMONT

HORIZON OUTLET CENTER

I-69 & I-80/90 Tollroad
Freemont, IN 46737
(800) 866-5900
(812) 833-1684
HOURS: Mon.-Sat. 9a.m.-9p.m., Sun. 11a.m.-6p.m.

AILEEN	219/833-4300
BANISTER SHOES	219/833-2755
BASS COMPANY STORE	219/833-2716
BASS SHOE	219/833-1104
BUBBA'S PIZZA	219/833-4311
BUGLE BOY	219/833-6720
CAPE ISLE KNITTERS	219/833-3235
CARTER'S CHILDRENSWEAR	219/833-6425
CHAUS	219/833-3008
COACH FACTORY STORE	219/833-1327
CORNING/REVERE	219/833-1572
FLORSHEIM SHOE	219/833-6244
FLUF N' STUF	NEW
GEOFFREY BEENE COMPANY STORE	219/833-6647
HIGH MOON CAFE	219/833-3897
HUSH PUPPIES FACTORY DIRECT	219/833-1026
JAYMAR FACTORY OUTLET	219/833-1100
JOCKEY	NEW
JONES NEW YORK	219/833-1121
KITCHEN COLLECTION	219/833-4150
LEATHER MANOR	219/833-2588

L'EGGS HANES BALI	219/833-3096
LESLIE FAY	219/833-3020
LEVI'S OUTLET BY DESIGNS	219/833-1417
LONDON FOG	NEW
OLGA/WARNER'S	219/833-4437
ONEIDA	219/833-1907
PAPER FACTORY	219/833-6424
POLO/RALPH LAUREN	219/833-6255
PRESTIGE FRAGRANCE	NEW
SOCKS GALORE	219/833-2590
SWEATSHIRT COMPANY	219/833-1783
TOTES/SUNGLASS WORLD	219/833-2388
TOY LIQUIDATORS	219/833-2933
VAN HEUSEN	219/833-4029
WELCOME HOME	219/833-2037
WESTPORT, LTD.	219/833-6225

INDIANAPOLIS

EASTGATE CONSUMER MALL
7150 E. Washington St.
Indianapolis, IN 46219
(317) 352-0951
HOURS: Mon.-Sat. 10a.m.-9p.m., Sun. 12a.m.-5p.m.

$5-10-15-20 PLACE	317/322-0757
ALL FOR ONE	317/353-6282
BEDDING LIQUIDATORS	317/353-2226
BOOKLAND	317/356-3921
BUILDERS SQUARE	317/356-3012
BURLINGTON COAT FACTORY	317/352-9166
COUNTRY SWEATS	317/353-8043
DUNHAM'S SPORTING GOODS	317/357-5300
ELAINE'S	317/357-8205
F&M DISTRIBUTORS	317/353-1003
FAMOUS FOOTWEAR	317/356-5513

GOLDEN CHAIN GANG	317/357-4102
HALL OF CARDS	317/353-6436
HIT OR MISS	317/356-9771
INDY TIRE	317/352-0168
JIFFY LUBE	317/353-0500
KITTLE'S CLEARANCE CENTER	317/359-6586
KITTLE'S FURNITURE FACTORY OUTLET	317/356-5400
LINENS 'N THINGS	317/353-1441
NATIONAL RECORD MART	317/356-8774
ROSEWOOD GALLERIES	317/352-0663
SHANE JEWELERS FACTORY OUTLET	317/357-0209
SIZES UNLIMITED	317/359-4455
SPORTS FANATICS	317/359-9789
THE FINISH LINE	317/353-6310
VILLAGE CLOCK SHOP	317/359-3462
WILD & WONDERFUL WESTERN WEAR	317/352-1564

MICHIGAN CITY

LIGHTHOUSE PLACE OUTLET CENTER

601 Wabash St.
Michigan City, IN 46360
(219) 879-6506
HOURS: Mon.-Sat. 9a.m.-8p.m., Sun. 10a.m.-6p.m.

9 WEST	219/879-1655
ADOLFO II	219/872-9388
ADRIENNE VITTADINI	219/874-2584
AILEEN	219/872-7117
ALL STARS	219/874-0014
AMERICAN TOURISTER	219/879-6730
ANKO ALSO	219/874-2831
ANNE KLEIN	219/879-5028
AUREUS	219/879-1238
BANISTER	219/872-0448
BASS SHOES	219/874-2142

BASS CLOTHING	219/873-1783
BENNETON	219/874-5827
BLACK ROSE JEWELRY	219/874-4740
BOOT FACTORY	219/874-0291
BOSTON TRADER	219/873-9529
BRANDS OUTLET & ALTERATIONS	219/872-6396
BROOKS BROS.	219/879-6777
BUGLE BOY	219/874-5667
BUXTON	219/879-6730
CAPE ISLE KNITTERS	219/873-9442
CARD FACTORY	219/879-1099
CAROLE LITTLE	219/872-4341
CARTER'S	219/874-4811
CHAMPION HANES	219/872-9254
CHAUS	219/874-5230
CHICO'S	219/872-8699
CLIFFORD & WILLS	219/873-9522
CORNING	219/879-0636
CRATE & BARREL	219/878-0200
DANSK	219/879-8300
DISCOUNT ENTERTAINMENT	219/873-1090
DONNA KARAN	219/874-7177
EAGLE'S EYE	219/879-6510
EDDIE BAUER	219/874-6178
ETIENNE AIGNER	219/879-0318
FAMOUS BRANDS ELECTRONICS	219/879-1192
FAMOUS BRANDS HOUSEWARES	219/879-0438
FANNY FARMER	219/872-8269
FIELDCREST/CANNON	219/874-2084
FLORENCE EISEMAN	219/879-1767
GEOFFREY BEENE	219/873-9527
HARVE´ BENARD	219/872-3566
HATHAWAY	219/879-4506
HE-RO GROUP	219/879-4237
HOT KNOTS	219/872-3594
HUSH PUPPIES	219/872-0809

IZOD FACTORY STORE	219/872-8695
J. CREW	219/873-9292
J.H. COLLECTIBLES	219/872-4661
JAYMAR	219/879-6336
JOCKEY	219/872-5700
JOHN HENRY & FRIENDS	219/879-6903
JONATHAN LOGAN	219/879-2422
JONES NEW YORK	219/874-8048
JONES NEW YORK EXECUTIVE SUITS	219/879-4789
JONES NEW YORK WOMAN	219/878-1002
KAREN'S ALTERATIONS	219/879-6336
KITCHEN COLLECTION	219/874-5854
LEATHER MANOR	219/879-6916
L'EGGS/HANES/BALI	219/879-5832
LEVI'S OUTLET	219/879-7950
LONDON FOG	219/872-0600
MAIDENFORM	219/874-3433
MIKASA	NEW
NICKELS COMPANY STORE	219/872-6848
OILILY	219/872-3577
OLGA/WARNER'S	219/874-6706
ONEIDA	219/879-6758
PAPER FACTORY	219/874-8447
PELICAN'S RESTAURANT	219/879-0935
PEPPERIDGE FARM	219/872-2205
PERFUMANIA	219/873-1122
POLO/RALPH LAUREN	219/874-9442
PRESTIGE FRAGRANCE	219/872-0977
PULLMAN CAFE & CLUB CAR	219/879-3393
REMINGTON	219/872-4955
RIBBON OUTLET	219/874-4953
ROYAL DOULTON	219/872-7916
S & K MENSWEAR	219/879-0331
SANDS OF TIME	219/874-9860
SARA LEE OUTLET	219/878-0114
SASSAFRAS	219/872-4112

SCOOPS ICE CREAM	219/872-6560
SIDE OUT	219/879-1446
SILVER SCREEN	219/879-1755
SOCKS GALORE & MORE	219/879-2244
STONE MOUNTAIN HANDBAG	219/873-0048
SUGAR PLUM COTTAGE	219/879-7117
SWEATSHIRT COMPANY	219/873-9540
SWEET PEA'S	219/873-0637
THE BOOKSTORE	219/879-3993
THE GOODSHIP	219/872-9477
TIES, ETC.	219/872-6661
TIVOLLI SQUARE	219/879-2400
TOTES	219/874-1350
TOY LIQUIDATORS	219/872-8882
VAN HEUSEN	219/879-6744
WALLET WORKS	219/872-4985
WELCOME HOME	219/879-6939
WEMCO	219/874-4434
WESTPORT LTD.	219/872-3213
WESTPORT WOMAN	219/873-9580

V
Directory of Catalogues

≺ARTS, CRAFTS, & HOBBIES≻

DANIEL SMITH ARTISTS MATERIALS

4130 First Ave. South
Seattle, WA 98134
800/426-6740
FREE

SAVINGS: Up to 57%
PRODUCTS: Artists materials including watercolors, oils, brushes, framing supplies, easels, and a variety of paper.

GETTINGER FEATHER CORP.

16 W. 36th St.
New York, NY 10018
212/695-9470
$2.00

SAVINGS: Up to 50%
PRODUCTS: Pheasant, turkey, duck, goose, rooster, ostrich feathers and more.

INDOOR GARDENING SUPPLIES

P.O. Box 40567
Detroit, MI 40567
313/668-8384
FREE

SAVINGS: Up to 40%
PRODUCTS: Indoor gardening supplies and accessories.

JAMESTOWN STAMP COMPANY
341-3 E. Third St.
Jamestown, NY 14701-0019
716/488-0763
FREE

SAVINGS: Competitive prices
PRODUCTS: Commemorative stamps, bank notes, sports cards, and albums.

LEATHER UNLIMITED CORP.
7155 Hwy. B, Dept. BR5
Belgium, WI 53004
414/994-9464
$2.00

SAVINGS: Competitive Prices
PRODUCTS: Leather purses, vests, belts, craft kits, and leather care products.

PEARL PAINT COMPANY
308 Canal St.
New York, NY 10013-2572
800/221-6845
FREE

SAVINGS: Up to 70%
PRODUCTS: Craft, graphic, and artists supplies.

SMILEY'S YARNS
92-06 Jamaica Ave.
Woodhaven, NY 11421
718/847-2185
FREE

SAVINGS: 25-75%
PRODUCTS: Name brands such as Pingouin, Patons, and Hayfield.

SUBURBAN SEW'N SWEEP

8814 Ogden
Brookfield, IL 60513
800/642-4056
FREE

SAVINGS: Competitive prices
PRODUCTS: Complete line of Singer and White sewing machines and sergers.

TAYLOR'S CUTAWAY & STUFF

2802 E. Washington St.
Urbana, IL 61801
FREE

SAVINGS: Up to 75%
PRODUCTS: Patterns and craft supplies.

THAI SILKS

252 State St.
Los Altos, CA 94022
800/221-SILK
415/948-8611
FREE

SAVINGS: Competitive prices
PRODUCTS: Scarves, shawls, fabric by the yard, neckties and silk garments.

THE BUTTON SHOP

7023 Roosevelt Rd.
Berwyn, IL 60402
708/795-1234
FREE

SAVINGS: 20 - 50%
PRODUCTS: Buttons, zippers, elastic, thread, and other notions.

THE FABRIC CENTER
485 Electric Ave.
Fitchburg, MA 01420
508/343-4402
$2.00

SAVINGS: Competitive prices
PRODUCTS: Top-quality home decorating fabrics

≺ BOOKS ≻

BARNES & NOBLE
126 Fifth Ave.
New York, NY 10011
800/242-6657
FREE

SAVINGS: Up to 80%
PRODUCTS: Best sellers, reference books, videos, and CD's.

DAEDALUS BOOKS
Box 9132
Hyattsville, MD 20781
800/395-2665
FREE

SAVINGS: Up to 89%
PRODUCTS: Books on all subjects.

JESSICA'S BISCUIT
Box 301
Newtonville, WA 02160
800/878-4264
$2.00

SAVINGS: 30% to 70%
PRODUCTS: Cookbooks from the likes of Julia Child and Wolfgang Puck

U.S. GOVERNMENT BOOKS

Superintendent of Documents
U.S. Government Printing Office
Washington, DC 20402-9325
FREE

PRODUCTS: Useful money saving consumer information on a variety of subjects for all ages.

< CLOTHING & PERSONAL PRODUCTS >

CHADWICK'S OF BOSTON

One Chadwick Place, Box 1600
Brockton, MA 02403-1600
508/583-6600
FREE

SAVINGS: 33% to 51%
PRODUCTS: Quality women fashions in a variety of styles.

ARCTIC SHEEPSKIN OUTLET

I-94 at Hammond Exit
Hammond, WI 54015
800/428-9276
FREE

SAVINGS: Competitive prices
PRODUCTS: Sheepskin slippers, hats, mittens, seatcovers, and rugs.

BEAUTIFUL VISIONS

810 S. Hicksville Rd.
Hicksville, NY 11855
516/567-0990
FREE

SAVINGS: Up to 90%
PRODUCTS: Name brand cosmetics and fragrances.

BEAUTY BOUTIQUE
6836 Engle Rd.
Cleveland, OH 44101-4519
216/86-1712
FREE

SAVINGS: Up to 90%
PRODUCTS: Nationally known cosmetics from brands such as Chanel, Christian Dior, Estee Lauder, and many more.

DESIGNER DIRECT
Designer Circle
Salem, VA 24156-0501
800/848-2929
FREE

SAVINGS: Up to 60%
PRODUCTS: Women's fashions, accessories, and footwear.

ESSENTIAL PRODUCTS CO., INC.
90 Water St.
New York, NY 10005
212/344-4288
FREE

SAVINGS: Up to 90%
PRODUCTS: Quality imitations of name brand and designer fragrances.

FASHION GALAXY
P.O. Box 26
Hanover, PA 17333-0227
717/633-3343
FREE

SAVINGS: Up to 75%
PRODUCTS: Womens fashions from sizes 6 to 26.

HIDALGO INC.

45 La Buena Vista
Wimberley, TX 78676
512/847-2177
800/786-2021
FREE

SAVINGS: 45% or more.
PRODUCTS: Eyewear including names such as Ray-Ban and Gargoyles.

ROSS-SIMONS JEWELERS

9 Ross-Simons Dr.
Cranston, RI 02920-9848
800/556-7376
FREE

SAVINGS: Competitive prices
PRODUCTS: Fine jewelry, flatware, china, crystal, silver, and collectibles.

SHOWCASE OF SAVINGS

P.O. Box 748
Rural Hall, NC 27098
910/744-1170
FREE

SAVINGS: Up to 65%
PRODUCTS: L'eggs, Hanes, Underalls, Isotoner, and Coloralls stockings and other undergarments.

SPORTSWEAR CLEARINGHOUSE
P.O. Box 317746Y2
Cincinnati, OH 45231
513/522-3511
FREE

SAVINGS: 60% and more
PRODUCTS: Shorts, T- shirts, sweatshirts and hats.

SUNGLASSES U.S.A.
469 Sunrise Hwy.
Lynbrook, NY 11563
800/USA-RAYS
$1.00

SAVINGS: Up to 33%
PRODUCTS: Ray-Ban sunglasses in a variety of styles.

THE DEERSKIN PLACE
283 Akron Rd.
Ephrata, PA 17522
717/733-7624
FREE

SAVINGS: 30% to 50%
PRODUCTS: Unique gifts including moccasins and handbags.

WINTER SILKS
2700 Laura Lane
Middleton, WI 53562
800/648-7455
FREE

SAVINGS: Competitive prices
PRODUCTS: Silk clothing for all seasons.

RUBENS & MARBLE, INC.
P.O. Box 14900-S
Chicago, IL 60614
312/348-6200
FREE

SAVINGS: Up to 60%
PRODUCTS: Baby shirts, sheets, stay-up stretch diapers, training panties, bibs, gowns, and kimonos.

≺ ENTERTAINMENT ≻

CABLE FILMS
P.O. Box 7171
Kansas City, MO 64113
913/362-2804
FREE

SAVINGS: Up to 30%
PRODUCTS: VHS or Beta film classics of the 20's, 30's, and 40's.

FORTY-FIVES
Box 358
Lemoyne, PA 17043-0358
$2.00

SAVINGS: Up to 50%
PRODUCTS: 45 RPM records priced between $1 and $2 based on their condition.

FREE THINGS FOR KIDS TO WRITE AWAY FOR
P.O. Box 85
Livingston, NJ 07039-0085
$2.00

PRODUCTS: Stickers, posters, games, sports cards, and more.

KICKING MULE RECORDS, INC.

P.O. Box 158
Alderpoint, CA 95411
800/262-5312
$1.00

SAVINGS: Up to 10%
PRODUCTS: Large selection of CD's, cassettes, books, videos, and instructional tapes.

RICK'S MOVIE GRAPHICS

P.O. Box 23709
Gainesville, FL 32602
800/252-0425
$3.00

SAVINGS: Competitive prices
PRODUCTS: 8x10 color photographs of celebrities and movie posters as low as $15.

≺ FOOD & BEVERAGE ≻

CAVIARTERIA INC.

29 E. 60th St.
New York, NY 10022
800/4-CAVIAR
FREE

SAVINGS: Up to 50%
PRODUCTS: Fresh Caspian Beluga, Oscetra, Sevruga caviar, smoked salmon, Foie Gras, and many other specialty foods.

JAFFE BROS. INC.
P.O. Box 636
Valley Center, CA 92082
619/749-1133
FREE

SAVINGS: Competitive prices
PRODUCTS: Natural and organic fruits, flour, sauces, and gourmet coffee.

UNITED PHARMACAL CO., INC.
Box 969
St. Joseph, MO 64502
816/233-8800
FREE

SAVINGS: Competitive prices
PRODUCTS: Complete pet supplies for your dog or cat.

VITAMIN CO-OP
44-823 Guadalupe Dr.
Indian Wells, CA 92210
619/341-1070
FREE

SAVINGS: 30% to 40%
PRODUCTS: Natural soaps, lotions, deodorants, shampoos, herbs and vitamins.

VITAMIN POWER, INC.
39 Saint Mary's Pl.
Freeport, NY 11520
800/645-6567
FREE

SAVINGS: Up to 51%
PRODUCTS: Vitamins, supplements, herbal teas, weight control, body-building programs, skin care, and health literature.

WINE LINK
420 Talbert St.
Daly City, CA 94014
800/231-1171
FREE

SAVINGS: 10% - 15%
PRODUCTS: Champagne, red, white, and dessert organic wines with low or no sulfites.

WOOD'S CIDER MILL
Rd. 2 Box 477
Springfield, VT 05156
802/263-5547
FREE

SAVINGS: Competitive prices
PRODUCTS: Cider jelly, boiled cider, cider and maple syrup.

≺ HOUSEHOLD GOODS & AUTOMOTIVE ≻

AAA-ALL FACTORY, INC.

1230 N. 3rd
Abilene, TX 79601
915/677-1311
$2.00

SAVINGS: Competitive prices.
PRODUCTS: Name brand vacuums. Call with model numbers and they'll give you a quote.

ABC VACUUM CLEANER WAREHOUSE

6720 Burnet Rd.
Austin, TX 78757
800/285-8145, 512/459-7643
FREE

SAVINGS: Up to 35%
PRODUCTS: Kirby, Filter Queen, Rainbow, Tri-Star, and Thermax

ADIRONDACK DESIGNS

350 Cypress St.
Fort Bragg, CA 95457
800/222-0343
FREE

SAVINGS: Competitive prices
PRODUCTS: Garden furniture and accessories constructed from redwwod.

AMERICAN DISCOUNT WALLCOVERINGS
1411 Fifth Ave.
Pittsburgh, PA 15219
800/777-2737
FREE

SAVINGS: Up to 70%
PRODUCTS: First quality wallcoverings, fabrics, and window treatments.

BARRONS
22790 Heslip Dr.
Novi, MI 48050
800/538-6340
FREE

SAVINGS: Up to 66%
PRODUCTS: Famous name-brand like Waterford, Baccarat, Mikasa, Noritaki, and Lenox china, crystal, and flatware.

BEVERLY BREMER SILVER SHOP
3164 Peachtree Rd. NE
Atlanta, GA 30305
404/261-4009
FREE

SAVINGS: Up to 75%
PRODUCTS: New and nearly new sterling silver flatware, hollowware, jewelry, collectibles, and gifts.

BRASS BEDS DIRECT

4866 W. Jefferson Blvd.
Los Angeles, CA 90016
800/727-6865
FREE

SAVINGS: Competitive prices
PRODUCTS: Brass beds, headboards, and footboards.

CRUTCHFIELD

1 Crutchfield Park
Charlottesville, VA 22906
800/446-1640
FREE

SAVINGS: Up to 44%
PRODUCTS: Car stereo systems, home audio and video, computers, telephones, facsimile machines and more.

DAMARK INTERNATIONAL

6707 Shingle Creek Pkwy.
Minneapolis, MN 55430
800/729-9000
FREE

SAVINGS: Up to 73%
PRODUCTS: Sony, Pioneer, Yamaha audio and video, furniture, exercise equipment, and tents.

DOMESTICATIONS
Box 40
Hanover, PA 17333
800/782-7722
$2.00

SAVINGS: Up to 57%
PRODUCTS: Name brand bedding, linen, towels, and window coverings.

GLOBAL VILLAGE IMPORTS
1101 S.W. Washington, #140
Portland, OR 97205
503/274-8778
$3.50

SAVINGS: Competitive prices
PRODUCTS: Hand-woven fabrics from Guatemala.

HIAWATHA HOMES
P.O. Box 1148
Pacific Palisades, CA 90272
310/454-4809

PRODUCTS: Architectural designs of single family homes.

INTERSTATE MUSIC SUPPLY
13819 W. National Ave.
New Berlin, WI 53151
800/837-BAND
FREE

SAVINGS: Up to 30%
PRODUCTS: Variety of musical instruments, carrying-cases, drums, musical clothing, repair parts and tools.

J. C. WHITNEY & CO.
P.O. Box 8410
Chicago, IL 60680
312/431-6102
FREE

SAVINGS: Up to 20%
PRODUCTS: Full line of automotive accessories, over 65,000 items.

JOHNSON'S CARPETS
3239 South Dixie Hwy.
Dalton, GA 30720
800/235-1079
404/277-2775
FREE

SAVINGS: Up to 80%
PRODUCTS: Dupont stainmaster, Weardated, vinyl, and wood flooring.

MIDAS CHINA & SILVER
5050 Nicholson Lane
Rockville, MD 20852
800/368-3153
FREE

SAVINGS: Up to 60%
PRODUCTS: Fine china and sterling flatware.

PORTER'S CAMERA STORE, INC.

P.O. Box 628
Cedar Falls, IA 50613
800/553-2001
$2.00

SAVINGS: 10% to 88%
PRODUCTS: Cameras, accessories, darkroom equipment, and novelty items, such as turning photos into magazine covers.

POST WALLCOVERING DISTRIBUTORS, INC.

2065 Franklin Rd.
Bloomfield Hills, MI 48302
800/521-0650
FREE

SAVINGS: Up to 75%
PRODUCTS: First quality wallcoverings. Call in with book and pattern number and they will give you a quote.

ROBINSON'S WALLCOVERINGS

222 West Spring St.
Titusville, PA 16354
814/827-1893
$0.50

SAVINGS: Competitive prices
PRODUCTS: First quality wallcoverings.

ROSS-SIMONS JEWELERS

9 Ross Simons Dr.
Cranston, RI 02920-9848
800/556-7376
FREE

SAVINGS: Up to 60%
PRODUCTS: Crystal, silver, and upholstered furniture.

SAM ASH MUSIC CORPORATION

124 Fulton Ave.
Hempstead, NY 11550
800/4 SAM-ASH
516/485-2151

SAVINGS: Competitive prices
PRODUCTS: Musical instruments and accessories.

SANZ INTERNATIONAL

P.O. Box 1794
High Point, NC 27261
910/882-6212
FREE

SAVINGS: 30% to 90%
PRODUCTS: Major brand wallcovering and fabrics.

SHAMA IMPORTS INC.

P.O. Box 2900
Farmington Hills, MI 48333
313/478-7740
FREE

SAVINGS: Competitive prices
PRODUCTS: Hand-embroidered crewels.

SHAR PRODUCTS COMPANY
2465 S. Industrial Hwy.
Ann Arbor, MI 48104
800/248-7427
FREE

SAVINGS: Up to 60%
PRODUCTS: String musical instruments, carrying cases, sheet music, and accessories.

SILVER WALLPAPER, INC.
3001-15 Kensington Ave.
Philadelphia, PA 19134
800/426-6600
215/426-7600
FREE

SAVINGS: Up to 66%
PRODUCTS: First quality wallpaper, call for a quote on your pattern.

SOBOL HOUSE OF FURNISHINGS
Richardson Blvd.
Black Mountain, NC 28711
704/669-8031
FREE

SAVINGS: 40 to 50%
PRODUCTS: Quality office and residential furniture including modern, 18th Century, and traditional styles.

TAPESTRY
P.O. Box 46
Hanover, PA 17333-0046
800/833-9333
FREE

SAVINGS: Up to 10%
PRODUCTS: Full line of decorator items from tables to area rugs.

WAREHOUSE CARPETS, INC.
Box 3233
Dalton, GA 30721
800/526-2229
FREE

SAVINGS: Up to 50%
PRODUCTS: Name brand carpets like Mohawk and Aladdin.

< SPORTING GOODS >

CAMPMOR
Box 999
Paramus, NJ 07653
800/525-4784
FREE

SAVINGS: 40% to 50%
PRODUCTS: Name brand camping supplies and clothing for men, women, and children.

E & B DISCOUNT MARINE
201 Meadow Rd.
Edison, NJ 08818-3138
800/523-2926
$5.00

SAVINGS: 25% to 46%
PRODUCTS: Clothing, inclement weather attire, water sports equipment, sailing supplies, flotation devices, and electrical supplies.

HOLABIRD SPORTS DISCOUNTERS
9008 Yellow Brook Rd., Rossville Industrial Park
Baltimore, MD 21237
410/687-6400
FREE

SAVINGS: Up to 64%
PRODUCTS: First quality tennis, squash, racquetball, badminton and paddleball racquets, shoes, and accessories.

OKUN BROTHERS SHOES
356 E. South St.
Kalamazoo, MI 49007
800/433-6344
FREE

SAVINGS: Up to 26%
PRODUCTS: Name brand men and women shoes from Reebok to Saucony.

OVERTON'S
P.O. Box 8228
Greenville, NC 27835-8228
800/334-6541
FREE

SAVINGS: Up to 25%
PRODUCTS: Waterskis, life jackets, navigation equipment, propellers, and all of your other boating needs.

< MISCELLANEOUS >

A TO Z LUGGAGE

4627 New Ultrecht Ave.
Brooklyn, NY 11219
800/342-5011
FREE

SAVINGS: Competitive prices
PRODUCTS: Full-line Samsonite luggage.

CURRENT

The Current Building
Colorado Springs, CO 80941
800/525-7170
FREE

SAVINGS: Up to 20%
PRODUCTS: Gift wrap, cards, stationery, and children's games/books.

NATIONAL CONTACT LENS CENTER

3527 Bonita Vista Dr.
Santa Rosa, CA 95404
800/326-6352
FREE

SAVINGS: Up to 70%
PRODUCTS: Original factory sealed soft contact lenses.

PHARMAIL

P.O. Box 1466
Champlain, NY 12919
518/298-4922
FREE

SAVINGS: Up to 80%
PRODUCTS: Discount mail-order prescription drugs.

RITEWAY HEARING AID CO.
Box 597635
Chicago, IL 60659
312/539-6620
FREE

SAVINGS: Up to 50%
PRODUCTS: High quality hearing aids and accessories.

ROCKY MOUNTAIN STATIONERY
11725 Co. Rd. 27.3
Dolores, CO 81323
303/565-8230
$1 Plus Double SASE

SAVINGS: Up to 50%
PRODUCTS: Pressed dried flower notecards, a collection of 12 cards per envelope.

VIKING DISCOUNT OFFICE PRODUCTS
P.O. Box 61144
Los Angeles, CA 90061-0144
800/421-1222
FREE

SAVINGS: Up to 81%
PRODUCTS: Everything from paper and pens, to office furniture and equipment.

VI
At
Your Fingertips

INDEX OF STORES

INDEX OF CATALOGUES

DON'T PAY RETAIL! DISCOUNT COUPON

DIVERSIONS

10%

OFF PURCHASE

MAY NOT BE VALID ON CERTAIN ITEMS. EXPIRES 12-31-96

DON'T PAY RETAIL! DISCOUNT COUPON

FURNITURE BARGAINS

PRESENT FOR SAVINGS

MAY NOT BE VALID ON CERTAIN ITEMS. EXPIRES 12-31-96

DON'T PAY RETAIL! DISCOUNT COUPON

TIFFANY LAWN & GARDEN

BUY 5 YARDS OF HARDWOOD BARK MULCH
& GET THE 6TH ONE *FREE*

MAY NOT BE VALID ON CERTAIN ITEMS. EXPIRES 09-30-95

DON'T PAY RETAIL! DISCOUNT COUPON

DIVERSIONS

10%

OFF PURCHASE

MAY NOT BE VALID ON CERTAIN ITEMS. EXPIRES 12-31-96

DON'T PAY RETAIL! DISCOUNT COUPON

FURNITURE BARGAINS

PRESENT FOR SAVINGS

MAY NOT BE VALID ON CERTAIN ITEMS. EXPIRES 12-31-96

DON'T PAY RETAIL! DISCOUNT COUPON

TIFFANY LAWN & GARDEN

BUY 5 YARDS OF HARDWOOD BARK MULCH
& GET THE 6TH ONE *FREE*

MAY NOT BE VALID ON CERTAIN ITEMS. EXPIRES 09-30-95

DON'T PAY RETAIL! DISCOUNT COUPON

RERUNS

20%

OFF PURCHASE WITH COUPON

MAY NOT BE VALID ON CERTAIN ITEMS. EXPIRES 12-31-96

DON'T PAY RETAIL! DISCOUNT COUPON

THE TOGGERY RESALE BOUTIQUE

10%

OFF PURCHASE TOTAL PURCHASE

MAY NOT BE VALID ON CERTAIN ITEMS. EXPIRES 12-31-96

DON'T PAY RETAIL! DISCOUNT COUPON

U.S. UNFINISHED FURNITURE FACTORY

10%

OFF PURCHASE

NOT VALID ON SALE ITEMS. EXPIRES 12-31-96

ACKNOWLEDGMENTS

I dedicate this book to my family and special friends whose support and encouragement in life have meant more than they know.

To my dad for suggesting this project and for his much-needed advice and friendship. I would also like to thank him for teaching me never to settle for less than I want in life.

To Mom and Skip for always being there with a pat on the back and beaming pride when things have gone well and encouragement when they haven't. I thank them for teaching me to appreciate what I have and never to take things for granted.

To my husband and friend, Ed, for quietly putting up with a ghost of a wife during this project. And to my daughters, Sarah and Katie, whose hugs and smiles helped keep things in perspective.

To Jennifer—I knew we could do it!

— Regina Miller

I would like to dedicate this book to my husband, Scott, for putting up with my absence and giving me the chance to explore new territory.

To my parents for the encouragement they have provided.

To my grandparents for always making me laugh.

Last but not least, I would like to thank my co-author for providing the opportunity to meet my match in wit and developing a new friendship.

— Jennifer Mixer

We would both like to thank Adam Michaels, Craig Driver and Second Byte Computers for pulling rabbits out of hats to keep this project going. We would also like to thank Tina Hacker and Trish Cornett for their many late nights of help.

— Regina & Jennifer

TO ORDER

DON'T PAY RETAIL!

Indiana's Discount Buying Guide

Ask for more copies at your local bookstore

or

Please enclose a check or money order payable for $19.95 per book to DON'T PAY RETAIL! (shipping and handling are already included).

Mail to: **DON'T PAY RETAIL!**
P.O. Box 47554
Indpls., IN 46247

Special pricing is available for 10 or more copies. Please inquire.

Thank You For Your Order!

____
Name

____
Address Apt. #

____
City State Zip

____
Phone Number (including area code)

Please send me ____ copies of DON'T PAY RETAIL!
Enclosed is my check or money order for $_____